Wisdom
for a
Young
CEO

D0203954

Library of Congress Control Number: 2003109196

ISBN 0-7624-2275-0

Cover photograph by Paul Rider
Cover design by Bill Jones
Interior design by Gwen Galeone
Text and organization by Deborah Yost
Edited by Greg Jones
Typography: AGaramond, Century Old Style, Bulldog,
Copperplate, and DINEngschrift

Publisher's Note: All quotes and letters within are used by permission.
All participants held the positions and job titles as noted at the time
of correspondence.

This book may be ordered by mail from the publisher.
Please include $2.50 for postage and handling.
But try your bookstore first!

Running Press Book Publishers
125 South Twenty-second Street
Philadelphia, Pennsylvania 19103-4399

Visit us on the web!
www.runningpress.com

WISDOM FOR A YOUNG CEO

INCREDIBLE LETTERS AND INSPIRING ADVICE FROM TODAY'S BUSINESS LEADERS

~

By Douglas Barry

RUNNING PRESS
PHILADELPHIA · LONDON

To my family and best friend, Steph.

CONTENTS

Introduction

When I was 12 years old (I am now 17), my lifelong dream of becoming an archaeologist faded before my eyes. It faded, in fact, when I watched a TV documentary about archaeologists and learned what they really do. Of course I knew that they excavated bones and artifacts from the past, but I never realized just what lengths they went through to find their prizes. Hours of labor in the sun, in the dirt, and sometimes even underwater, suddenly didn't seem like fun to me. I began to wonder if it might be better to just sit in a nice office and manage these archaeologists out in the field while I still got to reap the benefits of the dig. . . .

Around the same time, I started asking my mom

While touring the French countryside, I saw a McDonald's restaurant in the middle of a small village. I was speechless! And it struck me like a bolt of lightning—this awesome power of major corporations to influence the entire world . . . .

about what she did at work every day (she's a corporate executive) and actually listening to what she said. I would ask her questions about reports she was preparing and meetings she had attended, and what went on in those meetings. Eventually, I started to picture myself in such a position, realizing that, after all, I would definitely rather work with people than with a bunch of dirty old bones. And I even began to wonder if I could surpass the level that my mother had reached in her career.

Then, in the summer after I finished 7th grade, my family took a trip to Europe. While touring the French countryside, I saw a McDonald's restaurant in the middle of a small village. I was speechless! And it struck me like a bolt of lightning, this awesome power of major corporations to influence the entire world, even tiny villages in France. It was then that I decided to strive for the very best, and to reshape my future goals. It was then that I knew I wanted to become a Chief Executive Officer of a major corporation.

But soon panic set in. *How does one become a CEO?*, I wondered. Sure my mom is a corporate executive and my father is a doctor, but no one in our extended family has ever reached the heights of CEO of a major corporation. My first thought was that I had to raise my grade-point average from 3.9 to 4.0—otherwise, I thought, I would have no shot. I also figured I needed to join every club in school, and to be elected to the student-body government (no less than President would suffice, I figured).

But even as I began to set these enormous goals, I had a nagging feeling that perhaps I was missing some secret ingredient needed to become a CEO. So I decided to go directly to the source—to seek advice from the men and women who have reached the peak of the corporate mountain.

I prepared a letter in 2001 that I sent to the top executives of more than 150 major corporations (and I sent dozens more in 2003), asking them the basic question:

What does it take to become a CEO?

I could never have predicted what happened next. First of all, most of the CEOs responded with personal letters. And the responses I received were sincere, heartfelt, personal, and surprising! I quickly realized that my initial fears and subsequent plans (ensure a 4.0 GPA, join every club under the sun, become student-body president, etc.) were unfounded. And I found out that, besides the fact that there is no secret ingredient to becoming a CEO, there is also no prerequisite. The men and women who responded to my letter, and whose names we read about in newspapers every day, were themselves just kids once with big dreams. Many of them were not excellent students (though all appeared to be voracious readers). Most of them were not born with a silver spoon in their mouth. And all of them faced great adversity and achieved even greater accomplishments in their own unique ways.

But most of all, the similarity in the advice offered is what struck me most. Find something you love to do. Work hard. Respect others. Don't be afraid to fail. Protect your integrity. Go for your dreams. And more. . . .

The advice, personal counsel, and universal words of wisdom offered here by today's titans of industry has already inspired me immensely.

I hope it inspires you, too.

Passion

DO WHAT YOU LOVE; LOVE WHAT YOU DO

pas.sion (noun):
boundless enthusiasm
—American Heritage Dictionary, 3rd Edition

"I believe the people who are most successful are those who do what really interests them. There is no substitute for energy and enthusiasm."

—JACQUES A. NASSER, PRESIDENT AND CEO, FORD MOTOR COMPANY, DEARBORN, MI

Being a CEO is an awesome responsibility. It takes talent to get the job. It takes drive to keep up with the job. But what it takes to *be* the job is passion.

Passion for what they do is so great among the CEOs who wrote to me that I could practically feel their enthusiasm as I read their words. No wonder they took the time to write such meaningful and eloquent letters!

Passion, I learned, is not a fleeting emotion. It resonates from one being to everyone in hearing and feeling range, and then is passed along for everyone to experience. Passion is contagious. That is why it is so important for a leader to possess it, and to express it with great energy and consistency.

On Passion:

Enthusiasm, which, though founded neither on reason nor divine revelation, but rising from the conceits of a warmed or overweening brain, works yet, where it once gets footing, more powerfully on the persuasions and actions of men than either of those two, or both together: men being most forwardly obedient to the impulses they receive from themselves, and the whole man is sure to act more vigorously where the whole man is carried by a natural motion. For strong conceit, like a new principle, carries all easily with it when, got above common sense and freed from all restraint of reason and check of reflection, it is heightened into a divine authority, in concurrence with our own temper and inclination.

Though the odd opinions and extravagant actions enthusiasm has run men into were enough to warn them against this wrong principle, so apt to misguide them both in their belief and conduct: yet the love of something extraordinary, the ease and glory it is to be inspired and be above the common and natural ways of knowledge, so flatters many men's laziness, ignorance, and vanity that, when once they are got into this way of immediate revelation, of illumination without search, and of certainty without proof and without examination, it is a hard matter to get them out of it. Reason is lost upon them, they are above it; they see the light infused into their understandings, and cannot be mistaken: it is clear and visible there, like the light of bright sunshine, shows itself, and needs no other proof but its own evidence; they feel the hand of God moving them within and the impulses of the Spirit, and cannot be mistaken in what they feel. Thus they support themselves and are sure reason hath nothing to do with what they see and feel in themselves: what they have a sensible experience of admits no doubt, needs no probation. Would he not be ridiculous who should require to have it proved to him that the light shines and that he sees it? It is its own proof and can have no other. When the spirit brings light into our minds, it dispels darkness. We see it as we do that of the sun at noon, and need not the twilight of reason to show it us. This light from heaven is strong, clear, and pure, carries its own demonstration with it, and we may as rationally take a glow-worm to assist us to discover the sun as to examine the celestial ray by our dim candle, reason.

—JOHN LOCKE, FROM *ESSAY CONCERNING HUMAN UNDERSTANDING*

Johnson & Johnson

WILLIAM C. WELDON
CHAIRMAN
AND
CHIEF EXECUTIVE OFFICER

NEW BRUNSWICK, NEW JERSEY 08933

May 19, 2003

Mr. Douglas Barry

Voorhees, NJ 08043

Dear Douglas,

Thank you for your letter requesting important characteristics of a successful business person. I've been with Johnson & Johnson for over 30 years and have based my career on the following. I would advise students to take these attributes into consideration when venturing into the business world.

1. Be passionate about what you're doing. Be committed to it. Don't look over your shoulder and worry about the mistakes you've made, but determine how you can move forward.

2. Think positive! Worry about the things you can control and make sure you view them in a positive way. No matter what you look at, no matter how bad things look, there's always a positive side to it, and if you can keep yourself focused on the positive, and you can keep driving things in that direction, you'll always do well.

3. Be committed to be the best you can be. You can't like finishing second or losing. You've got to like winning. Never give up.

4. Be selective about where you work, and make sure you're comfortable with what the company stands for, what it represents, and that it's something you can really commit yourself to.

Douglas, I hope this answers your questions and is helpful to you Good luck to you in the future.

Sincerely,

William C. Weldon

William C. Weldon

"One thing I learned . . . is that I could never take a job simply because it might look good on my resume. I have to do things I enjoy."

—RAYMOND V. GILMARTIN, CHAIRMAN, PRESIDENT AND CEO, MERCK & CO., WHITEHOUSE STATION, NJ

"It's more about your passion, drive, and belief in yourself than it is about your intellect, who you know, or good luck."

—ROGER VALINE, CEO, Vision Service Plan, Sacramento, CA

"PASSIONATE PEOPLE GET THINGS DONE. PASSION FOR DOING WHAT YOU'RE CALLED TO DO RESONATES IN EVERY FIBER OF A TRUE LEADER. PASSION SHOWS. PASSIONATE PEOPLE ENERGIZE OTHER PEOPLE AND BUILD ENTHUSIASM. AND AS YOU SURELY KNOW, ENTHUSIASM IS CONTAGIOUS."

—LEONARD ROBERTS, Chairman and CEO, RadioShack Corp., Fort Worth, TX

Jacques A. Nasser
President and
Chief Executive Officer

Ford Motor Company
The American Road
P.O. Box 1899
Dearborn, Michigan 48121-1899 USA

January 28, 2000

Mr. Douglas Barry

Voorhees, New Jersey 08043

Dear Mr. Barry:

Thank you for your interest in my thoughts on achieving success.

As a boy, I was fascinated with world affairs, international business and cars. So working for a global auto company was a natural for me.

I believe the people who are most successful are those who do what really interests them. I also believe in valuing the differences among people, and working as a team. Differences in cultures and backgrounds provide learning experiences for individuals, and advantages for teams. I've had assignments on five continents for Ford, and I've seen the power of people of different backgrounds working together toward a common goal.

The people who have the greatest chance of being successful are those who work hard and are excited about what they are doing. There is no substitute for energy and enthusiasm. Success is for those who know what they want and go after it, no mater how difficult the path.

Thank you for your letter. Good luck in achieving your future goals.

Sincerely,

"Education will prepare you for anything in life, honesty is one of the primary and necessary ingredients, and a sincere love of what you're doing is the fuel that makes it all run."

—SUMMERFIELD K. JOHNSTON, JR., CEO, COCA-COLA ENTERPRISES, ATLANTA, GA

"Working hard and enjoying it are not only compatible but essential for long-term success."

—H.A. WAGNER, Chairman and CEO, Air Products and Chemicals Inc., Allentown, PA

People follow people who care about what they are doing. You've got to show people you have passion. You've got to be prepared to open up and say, 'I believe this.'

—MARK HARRIS, COUNTRY GENERAL MANAGER, IBM SOUTH AFRICA

"WE STARTED THE COMPANY ON A WING AND A PRAYER AND WANTED TO MAKE BOARDSHORTS, STAY NEAR THE BEACH, KEEP SURFING AND HAVE SOME FUN. MY CAREER JUST HAPPENED. I DIDN'T PREMEDITATE THIS. I THINK IT WAS MY NATURAL INSTINCT OF BEING AN ENTREPRENEUR. BEING HONEST, BEING LOYAL TO WORKERS AND FRIENDS AND ASKING OF PEOPLE HAS LED ME TO GOOD LEADERSHIP."

—BOB MCKNIGHT, Chairman of the Board, Quiksilver, Huntington Beach, CA

"You must be better than a good communicator—you must be a translator of dreams, a demonstrator of passion for pursuing the dream . . . ."

—ROSEMARIE B. GRECO, Director, Office of Health Care Reform, Harrisburg, PA

"EMBARK ON A CAREER WHERE YOU CAN NOT ONLY BE GOOD, BUT BE GREAT. [IT] MUST BE SOMETHING THAT COMES NATURALLY TO YOU, WHERE YOU HAVE A GIFT, AND THAT YOU LOVE."

—STEVE ODLAND, Chairman, President and CEO, Auto Zone Inc., Roseland, NJ

Truth to Self
the Best Motive

"First, what are you good at? Second, what do you really like to do? When you discover something that truly answers both of those questions, go for it. You will like getting up in the morning and going to work. You will probably be extremely effective at what you do. You will be noted by others because of your effectiveness and the positive attitude you bring to every day's task. When those things happen you have a good life and you will have maximized the chances that someone will take an aggressive interest in you and help you to move forward step by step."

—THOMAS S. JOHNSON, Chairman and CEO,
GreenPoint Bank, New York, NY

AIR PRODUCTS

Air Products and Chemicals, Inc.
7201 Hamilton Boulevard
Allentown, PA 18195-1501

H. A. Wagner
Chairman and
Chief Executive Officer

10 February 2000

Mr. Douglas Barry

Voorhees, NJ 08043

Dear Douglas:

Thank you for your letter of January 14, 2000. I apologize for being a bit tardy in my response.

Honesty and integrity are far and away the most important qualities any successful leader must have. These qualities are particularly important for a company CEO in today's fast changing, highly competitive business environment. Your employees, customers, and shareholders must have complete confidence in your statement and commitments.

Effective leaders are good communicators. You should work to develop good communication skills and <u>become a good listener</u>. Failure often results when leaders do not communicate clearly in language understood by their audience, and they are certain to fail if they ignore input from colleagues and direct reports.

The business world today is highly competitive and potentially stressful. Find a profession (engineer, financial analyst, etc.) that is compatible with your skills and interests and seek out a company that feels comfortable. Working hard and enjoying it are not only compatible but essential for long-term success. Ask yourself the question "Am I having fun working?", which is quite different from the question "Am I having fun at work?"

Those are just a few insights. I have enclosed a copy of our annual report and a brochure entitled "Our Fundamentals...Our Future", which talks about the important ingredients that have defined success for Air Products and Chemicals.

Your resume is very impressive. You have an excellent start and I expect you're getting some good coaching from both Mom and Dad. Good luck to you in your future and make sure you're having fun along the way.

Regards,

H A Wagner
H. A. Wagner

HAW/nab
Enclosures (2)

A Responsible Care® Company

"HARD WORK, OF COURSE, IS CRITICAL. BUT YOU HAVE TO BALANCE THAT WITH TIME FOR YOUR FAMILY AND FRIENDS. ONE-DIMENSIONAL PEOPLE ARE RARELY SUCCESSFUL OVER THE LONG HAUL."

—G. RICHARD THOMAN, President, Xerox Corporation, Stamford, CT

"THERE'S MORE TO LIFE THAN BEING A CEO, BUT GO FOR YOUR DREAMS WHATEVER THEY ARE."

—GEORGE M.C. FISHER, Chairman, Eastman Kodak Co., Rochester, NY

"ONE CAUTION—DO WHAT MAKES YOU HAPPY! DO NOT CHOOSE A DIRECTION OR A VOCATION BECAUSE OF MONEY. YOU WILL ONLY GET ONE TIME AROUND IN LIFE, AND YOU SHOULD ENJOY ALL OF YOUR EXPERIENCES, NOT JUST YOUR PAYDAY."

—ERROLL B. DAVIS JR., Chairman, President and CEO, Alliant Energy Corp., Madison, WI

"IT'S NOT ENOUGH TO BE SKILLED EXECUTIVES AND WORLD-CLASS MAN-
AGERS. TO BE TRUE LEADERS, WE NEED THE PASSION OF OUR DREAMS
AND A VISION OF HOW TO MAKE THEM REAL. PASSION THAT BURNS FROM
THE INSIDE OUT IS WHAT MAKES US REAL AND BELIEVABLE TO THOSE WE
WOULD LEAD. PASSION DRAMATIZES OUR COMMITMENT TO OUR COMMUNI-
TIES AND OUR CONSTITUENCIES."

—JUDITH RODIN, President, University of Pennsylvania, Philadelphia, PA

"BE PASSIONATE ABOUT WHAT YOU'RE DOING. BE COMMITTED TO IT. . . ."

—WILLIAM C. WELDON, Chairman and CEO, Johnson & Johnson, New Brunswick, NJ

"Develop a strong sense of personal responsibility and independence. Learn to get up and get started every morning."

—**ROY W. HALEY**, CEO, WESCO INTERNATIONAL, PITTSBURGH, PA

EXPRESS SCRIPTS®
Charting the Future of Pharmacy

June 25, 2003

Mr. Douglas Barry

Voorhees, NJ 08043

Dear Douglas:

Received your letter dated June 10, 2003. I appreciate your interest.

Becoming a CEO should not be your dream, or your goal -- even if you would like to be a CEO. Your dream should be to do good work, work that has real meaning to you and would help others. Then, if you find something you really do well, you will be on the right track. Maybe you'll be a CEO -- or maybe you'll be something else -- but in any case you will have a good life. There was no one turning point in my career.

Sincerely,

Barrett A. Toan
Chairman and Chief Executive Officer

13900 Riverport Drive . Maryland Heights, MO 63043 . www.express-scripts.com

BARNES&NOBLE
BOOKSELLERS

January 17, 2000

Mr. Doulgas Barry

Vorhees, NJ 08043

Dear Douglas:

To answer your question directly, the major qualities I believe I possess in abundance are:

- <u>Curiosity:</u> from which my intelligence and creative capabilities have been spawned.
- <u>Empathy:</u> I try to hear things through the ears of others, and see things through their eyes.
- <u>Determination:</u> I am very intense and focused, especially on problem solving. I also believe I am very objective, and never let my ego interfere with my thought processes.
- <u>Sense of Humor:</u> I never take myself too seriously, and I oftentimes look at myself and this world as a distant observer. Believe me, there is a lot to laugh about.

Mostly though, I believe I am successful because I have great parents and have had great mentors (see article). It seems obvious to me from your letter that you are similarly blessed.

Finally, my passion, too, is writing! I believe writing is the most important thing we do. I like to say that language is the programming of the mind. To me, good writers are the programmers of our civilization.

Oops, I forgot to answer your question on leadership. Here goes:

Leadership is something which should be inferred to one by their subordinates and their peers – not bestowed upon them by their masters. This attribute comes from the heart, soul, and spirit of a human being. It is difficult to define, but easy to recognize.

Are you a leader?

Sincerely,

Leonard Riggio

Leonard Riggio

LR/jlr
Encl.

cc: Mary Ellen Keating

Psst: Some CEO's write their own letters!

MENTORING U.S.A. ESSAY
By:
Leonard Riggio
Chairman & Chief Executive Officer
Barnes & Noble, Inc.

I am fortunate to have had three great mentors, each of whom have had a profound impact on my life: My father, Steve Riggio; my co-worker and friend, Hamilton Dolly; and my first and only "boss," Al Zavelle.

Steve Riggio was one of seven children who grew up in a tightly knit Italian-American family in little Italy in Manhattan. He was a brilliant man and a great athlete. Eventually, he became a highly ranked prizefighter whose claim to fame was in twice defeating Rocky Graziano, who had never been beaten twice before.

Dad did not like to lose anymore than he liked to get hit. After eighty-five professional fights, he left the ring without a scar on his face, and, unlike most prizefighters, he never slurred his words. He remained handsome and brilliantly articulate for the rest of his life. He saw boxing as both a science and an art -- studying and practicing like no one else in the game. He won because he out-boxed and out-trained his opponents. The power of his will was amazing.

Dad was completely focused on the relationship between mind and body, believing that the health of one would improve the health of the other. He drew his strength from his brain, and nourished his mind from the underpinnings of a sound body. Even later, when he became a cab driver, he would always work out. At traffic lights, he would get out of the cab and do deep knee- bends and push-ups. Other cabbies thought he was crazy – but they never told him to his face.

I played a lot of sports growing up and was close to the best kid on the block or on the team at most things I played. Much of it was due to the countless hours I spent at practice and the hustle I brought to the game. To this extent, I was a model for dad's beliefs: I was dedicated, focused, and relentless.

Surprisingly, for a boxer, dad believed in weight training for most sports. He was thirty years ahead of his time in thinking basketball players and golfers should lift weights. Back in the early Fifties, he also preached to my grandmother about working out. He was convinced that senior citizens could extend their life expectancy and add to their self esteem with a simple physical fitness routine. To this extent, he was the consummate optimist. His enthusiasm and energy inspired everyone he met.

Steve Riggio also believed a sound and active mind needed work and practice. He worked his mind as hard as he did his body. He never felt that people were born smarter than he was, and he easily made up for environmental deficiencies by his lifelong curiosity and intuition. Although he never graduated high school, dad completed the New York Times crossword puzzle nearly every day. "The pen is mightier than the sword," he would say. "Wars are nothing more than the battles over different ideas."

But, mentoring to him was not making his children into clones of himself. He gave me the resolve to live by the courage of my own convictions – not his beliefs. He rarely tried to rein me in – preferring to let me develop my own set of values and navigation system. The only thing he ever offered, which was close to an admonition, was this: "There is nothing in this world you can't do, and nothing in this universe you can't become, if you put your mind to it." He'd also qualify this a bit and say, "Hitch your wagon to a star and you'll never land short of the moon." For those who later described me as having "humble beginnings," they never met my dad and mentor, Steve Riggio.

High aspirations and indomitable will were also the attributes of my mentor, friend, and co-worker, Hamilton Dolly. More than any other person before or since, Hamilton opened up my eyes to the bigger world around me, purging forever my provincial inclinations and encouraging, even exhorting, me to fulfill my own destiny.

Growing up in Brooklyn during the McCarthy era, my world was colored with ignorant misconceptions and outright paranoia. Just years removed from the greatest atrocities in the history of the world, the fires of prejudice burned ever brightly in America. Union activists were considered communists; Jews were viewed with suspicion and distrust; and African-Americans were treated as second-class citizens. Although dad was a brilliant and compassionate man, his own worldview was shaped by his limited exposure; he could not, alone, expose me to the next level I so sorely needed.

Working alongside Hamilton Dolly at the New York University Bookstore, I was literally bombarded with conflicting and hopelessly complex points of view. Nothing in my past provided context for the issues I needed to resolve. During these formative years, Hamilton was my mentor and my beacon. He was, without a doubt, the most brilliant person I ever encountered. His mind was as fit and as hard and as facile as dad's considerable physique.

As manager of the textbook department, Hamilton took it upon himself to conduct a character-building school for the young people he

2

supervised. He believed, as dad did, that "indefatigable" effort could overcome environmental shortcomings. He lived and taught by what for him was a necessary principle: "It's <u>not</u> who you know – but what you know and what you do which creates success." He thought people should be connected to themselves before worrying about "connecting" to other people.

Hamilton always did, and continues to, believe that good work is its own reward. He instilled pride and dignity and purpose in the hundreds of people, largely from minority groups, that he trained. He was a role model in providing examples of how to act – but he was a brilliant mentor in teaching people how to think.

The NYU Bookstore also provided me with Al Zavelle, my first and only "boss." *"Mr. Zavelle"* was the very first symbol of authority I encountered in the real world outside of my home, but, fortunately for me, he represented the high mindedness necessary to be a great leader. He taught me what he knew by example and by explanation. To this day, he continues to write me useful notes and kind words of encouragement. Mentoring, to him, is clearly a lifetime commitment.

Understanding the importance of rationalizing the intersections between responsibility and authority, he took the work of managing a bookstore most seriously. In fact, he was the first college bookstore manager in America, to whom the title "Director" was conferred, because he made the business of selling textbooks to college students an all-encompassing mission. Not satisfied with being just another administrator, he considered himself part of the faculty, and his role as critical in the process of education. I owe to him the concept of bringing a missionary zeal to the workplace.

Over the course of his lifetime, Al Zavelle always broke the mold, because he was never satisfied with the status quo. Back in the days when computers were a primitive technology, he oversaw the complete automation of the NYU Bookstore's elaborate inventory management system – a feat which would not be duplicated for five years after we were up and running. A study in self-improvement, he earned his MBA in night school, while working as Bookstore Director during the day. Naturally, he was a straight *"A"* student, because the man simply would not accept mediocrity in anything he ever attempted.

On one occasion, as Mr. Zavelle was conducting a tour of the school supply section I managed, he came to a spot on the shelves where a certain brand of typing paper used to sit. "What's that?" he said. "That's the 409-IP," I replied. "It's on order." At this point, he pointed to the empty space angrily and said, "I don't give a damn about what is on order – our students can't type their homework on your excuses." Although this

3

stinging retribution spoiled my otherwise pleasant day, I have prospered since by remembering its message: Excuses are often the fine line between successful people and those who are victims of their own lack of resolve.

To this day, our college bookstore company, which now consists of more than three hundred stores, operates under this single admonition, thanks to the genius of Al Zavelle: "Cover thy shelves."

Steve Riggio, Hamilton Dolly, and Al Zavelle were three heroic figures in my life and three great mentors. My life was clearly nourished by what they contributed, and their lives were to some extent enriched by what I have achieved. Mentoring is all about the nurturing relationship between mentor and mentoree: each growing because of the other. Although there can be a profound difference between mentors and heroes, some individuals embody the greatness of both.

* * * * * * * * * * * * * * * *

Follow Your Heart

Q: Was there a turning point in your career that brought you down the path to become the leader you are today?

A: After graduating college, I worked for 14 years with a CPA firm where I became a partner. Somewhere around that time, I recognized that although I liked what I did and thought I was good at it, it was not what I wanted to do for the next 20+ years. So, I overcame my insecurities, my concern about my ability to succeed in a new environment, and changed positions and careers (sort of, as I became a CFO). From then on I always had confidence in my ability to face new challenges and take opportunities. I, at best, vaguely understood what was happening at the time of the decision.

—ARTHUR F. WEINBACH, CHAIRMAN and CEO,
AUTOMATIC DATA PROCESSING INC.,
ROSELAND, NJ

John W. Rowe
Chairman and CEO

Exelon Corporation
P.O. Box 805398
Chicago, Illinois 60680-5398

www.exeloncorp.com

July 22, 2003

Mr. Douglas Barry

Voorhees, NJ 08043

Dear Mr. Barry,

Thank you for your fascinating letter. You are very well spoken for someone so young, and I was delighted to read of your quest to communicate with CEO's around the country. Though it has taken me some time to write back, I am very interested in sharing some of my thoughts with you.

I was raised on a farm in southwestern Wisconsin, not too far from the metropolitan area where I now live, but my life there was very different from the one I lead now. My parents were formed by the Depression, and I was raised to believe that all good things are undeserved. Because I still maintain that outlook, I focus closely on the problems confronting my companies, and try to deal with them squarely. Because of this focus, my companies have become quite successful under my leadership.

A turning point in my career was when I first had a chance to become the CEO at Central Maine Power. The Board there was concerned that I was too young and inexperienced, so I drove to Maine and visited every town in which one of the directors lived. I came to not only know the geographic area, but was able to demonstrate to them that I took this job seriously and would take the necessary steps to prove my commitment to the Board.

I believe that my success has come because I am always aware, and thus, always balancing economics, politics and law. I strongly recommend you read J. Willard Hurst's book Law and Markets in US History. My fascination with history has helped me to manage many opportunities that current management gurus seem to just be discovering.

I am interested, too, in your compilation of responses. As an additional source of information, I refer you to the Arthur W. Page Society, who is publishing a compendium of letters from CEO's of America's best managed companies. I am enclosing my biography and a reading list that you may also find useful.

Regards,

John W. Rowe

90 Park Avenue
New York, NY 10016-1303

Thomas S. Johnson
Chairman and CEO

June 10, 2003

Mr. Douglas Barry

Voorhees, NJ 08043

Dear Mr. Barry:

I am pleased to respond to your letter regarding the role of the corporate CEO. The first thing I would say to you is that setting out with a desire to become CEO may not be the right approach. No matter how talented you are, no matter how hard you work, no matter what kind of advice you get from people, it is nearly impossible to foresee the twists and turns in a person's life and career and predict a route that is likely to lead him or her to any particular long-term goal. What is important, I think, is to have a general understanding of two things. First, what are you good at? Second, what do you really like to do? When you discover something that truly answers both of those questions, go for it.

If you go for a career in an area that meets the two criteria I mentioned, a lot of good things will happen to you. You will like getting up in the morning and going to work. You will probably be extremely effective at what you do. You will be noted by others because of your effectiveness and the positive attitude you bring to everyday's task. When those things happen you have a good life and you will have maximized the chances that someone will take an aggressive interest in you and help you to move forward step by step. That is the way it happened with me and I have seen that happen with many others.

There have been two major turning points in my working life. The first happened after my first 10 years at Chemical Bank. During the first 10 years I was in various staff positions and ultimately Chief Financial Officer. In 1979, at a time when there was tremendous turmoil in the capital markets, I was asked to take over the treasury division of Chemical Bank. I did not have nearly the experience that one would ideally have wanted to have, but since I had been willing to do everything that I had been asked to do up to that time, people trusted me and knew that I would be careful and honest. That led me for the first time to a top management position, responsible for a lot of risk and a lot of people and ultimately it led me to the presidency of the bank.

Another turning point occurred after the merger of Manufacturer's Hanover and Chemical Bank. For two years I was out of work because I was sort of the "odd person out" in the merger. When I went back to work at GreenPoint I entered a completely different type of business. Up until that time I had concentrated on commercial banking activities. At GreenPoint, I found myself leading a company that is a mass market retailer of financial services. The same kind of leadership skills are required, but at GreenPoint those skills are applied in a context dramatically different from commercial banks and I had to learn, starting at the age of 51, lots of new things. That was a renewal experience, and I think it gave me much more energy in the years ahead. I am very grateful that it happened to me.

I hope these comments are helpful to you. I wish you every success, but I wish it for you one step at a time, and if you don't wind up being a CEO, but do wind up happy, that is what is important.

Yours very sincerely,

What I've Learned

My parents always tell me that work isn't work if you like to do it.

S till, the biggest concern I have had about work is that it seems almost impossible to find a career that does not compromise your interests. But the more I learn, the more I realize that being successful isn't about making money or driving a luxury car to work every morning. One of the most important messages found in the letters I received from CEOs is that a successful person is one who finds fulfillment in every aspect of their lives and applies themselves to the best of their abilities to a task that is worthy of their time and effort. Being a CEO is not what makes the men and women who wrote to me successful. They are CEOs and leaders because what they love to do has made them successful human beings.

The problem that faces today's generation (excuse me for the generalization) is that we fear that success in the corporate world will mean we sold ourselves short for a bigger paycheck and status. What I've learned from these executives' letters, however, is that if you apply yourself to something that means a great deal to you, then you will not have to worry about "selling out." Your success, whether it be material or abstract, will simply be an added bonus to the joy you receive from doing what you love to do. Mr. Gilmartin of Merck verified my reluctance to compromise my beliefs and true passions for money, when he said he couldn't work for a bigger paycheck alone: "I have to do things I love," he said. It has been made clear through many of these letters that it is hard for one to go through life and do things only for the money. Happiness and success come from following your dreams, always keeping in mind that the dream you started out with can never be compromised along your journey.

Respect

MAKE PEOPLE YOUR PRIORITY

re.spect **(tr. verb):**
to feel or show deferential regard for
—American Heritage Dictionary, 3rd Edition

"I try to hear things through the ears of others, and see things through their eyes."

—LEONARD RIGGIO, CHAIRMAN AND CEO, BARNES & NOBLE, INC., NEW YORK, NY

I s it lonely at the top? Not according to the CEOs I heard from! Great CEOs recognize that they cannot do their jobs alone. They depend on others to help make their company prosper—and this includes every single person who is a part of the organization. A great CEO listens to others, feels their concerns, delegates authority, and nurtures the company's talent. As so many of the CEOs who wrote me noted: It's all about people.

On Respect:

It is not by wearing down into uniformity all that is individual in themselves, but by cultivating it, and calling it forth, within the limits imposed by the rights and interests of others, that human beings become a noble and beautiful object of contemplation; and as the works partake the character of those who do them, by the same process human life also becomes rich, diversified, and animating, furnishing more abundant aliment to high thoughts and elevating feelings, and strengthening the tie which binds every individual to the race, by making the race infinitely better worth belonging to. In proportion to the development of his individuality, each person becomes more valuable to himself, and is therefore capable of being more valuable to others. There is a greater fullness of life about his own existence, and when there is more life in the units there is more in the mass which is composed of them. As much compression as is necessary to prevent the stronger specimens of human nature from encroaching on the rights of others cannot be dispensed with; but for this there is ample compensation even in the point of view of human development. The means of development which the individual loses by being prevented from gratifying his inclinations to the injury of others, are chiefly obtained at the expense of the development of other people. And even to himself there is a full equivalent in the better development of the social part of his nature, rendered possible by the restraint put upon the selfish part. To be held to rigid rules of justice for the sake of others, develops the feelings and capacities which have the good of others for their object. But to be restrained in things not affecting their good, by their mere displeasure, develops nothing valuable, except such force of character as may unfold itself in resisting the restraint. If acquiesced in, it dulls and blunts the whole nature. To give any fair play to the nature of each, it is essential that different persons should be allowed to lead different lives. In proportion as this latitude has been exercised in any age, has that age been noteworthy to posterity. Even despotism does not produce its worst effects, so long as individuality exists under it; and whatever crushes individuality is despotism, by whatever name it may be called, and whether it professes to be enforcing the will of God or the injunctions of men.

—JOHN STUART MILL, FROM *ON LIBERTY*

Erroll B. Davis Jr.
Chairman, President and
Chief Executive Officer

Alliant Energy Corporation
4902 North Biltmore Lane
P.O. Box 77007
Madison, WI 53707-1007

July 7, 2003

Mr. Douglas Barry

Voorhees, NJ 08043

Dear Mr. Barry:

Thanks for your kind and fascinating note of June 20th. By its content and your resume, I can tell that you are well on your way to being quite successful in life's pursuits. Let me see, however, if I might address your questions.

On the first question, I am not sure that there was a particular turning point in my career that got me to where I am today. I suggest to most young people that life is not a "big bang theory" or a string of incredible successes—one following another. Life is always a series of ups and downs, triumphs and failures. You may be successful if your triumphs simply outnumber your failures. But, in order to be successful, you must experience those failures and you must learn from them.

On the second point, I suspect you have much of what you need already to become a leader. My sense is that leaders lead because people are willing to follow. And people are willing to follow for some very simple reasons. First, no one will follow you if you don't treat them with dignity and respect. No one will follow you if they do not understand where you are going, so you must be open and communicative with them. No one will follow you if they do not trust you; therefore, you must be honest at all times. You must communicate the bad, as well as the good.

No one will follow you if you do not listen to his or her concerns. Of all of the skills I think people fall short on, it is the skill of listening. You are, of course, well ahead of the game here because you are seeking out the advice of others. No one will follow you if they feel that they are insignificant. Therefore, it is important to make sure that everyone whom you are privileged to lead understands their role and is also made to understand the importance of that role. People should also be held accountable. This will engender respect as well.

And lastly, the surest way to lose the right to lead is to be abusive of people. Holding people accountable and having a sense of discipline is very different than being abusive. Abusive implies a lack of respect for the individual and for his or her capabilities.

Again, I hope my thoughts are helpful to you in your quest to become a leader. Continue to do well in school, and continue to focus on your objectives. One caution — Do what makes you happy! Do not choose a direction or a vocation because of money. You will only get one time around in life, and you should enjoy all of your experiences, not just your payday.

Best wishes for continued success!

Regards,

Erroll B. Davis, Jr.
Chairman, President & CEO

"I HAVE FOUND THAT THE TWO BEST QUALITIES A CEO CAN HAVE ARE THE ABILITY TO LISTEN AND TO ASSUME THE BEST MOTIVES IN OTHERS."

—JACK M. GREENBERG, Chairman and CEO, McDonalds Corp., Oak Brook, IL

"It's all about people. Too much is focused on leadership activities. But great leaders inspire followership!"

—STEVE ODLAND, Chairman, President and CEO, Auto Zone Inc., Roseland, NJ

"FIRST, NO ONE WILL FOLLOW YOU IF YOU DON'T TREAT THEM WITH DIGNITY AND RESPECT. NO ONE WILL FOLLOW YOU IF THEY DO NOT TRUST YOU; THEREFORE, YOU MUST BE HONEST AT ALL TIMES. YOU MUST COMMUNICATE THE BAD, AS WELL AS THE GOOD."

—ERROLL B. DAVIS JR., Chairman, President and CEO, Alliant Energy, Madison, WI

FIRST TENNESSEE

All Things Financial.

J. Kenneth Glass
President & Chief Executive Officer

June 2, 2003

Mr. Douglas Barry

Voorhees, NJ 08043

Dear Douglas:

Thank you for your letter inquiring about becoming a CEO.

My advice to young people who hope to be a CEO or President of a company some day is rather basic. First, treat people right and fairly. Give people the tools they need to do the job and the authority to use them. They will generally surprise you.

Second, groups working together produce better results than individuals. Be a part of a team and be cooperative. Be a team player.

Third, surround yourself with capable people who will challenge your ideas and decisions.

Fourth, and my favorite, is honesty and hard work are still the key to success. Do not stay in a work or social environment where you are not encouraged to do what is right. Be diligent about what you do and do not be impatient about advances and promotions. Focus on your skills and being you and not on being CEO.

Good luck to you in your career.

Ken Glass

First Tennessee Bank National Association
P.O. Box 84
Memphis, TN 38101-0084

Cable FIRBANK

January 21, 2000

Mr. Douglas Barry

Voorhees, New Jersey 08043

Dear Douglas:

What a pleasure to hear from such an ambitious young man as you! It is good that you are already giving some thought to your long-range goals.

You asked for three (3) qualities that best prepared me for becoming the CEO of First Union National Bank. From my personal experiences, the qualities that helped me in achieving my goals include:

- **<u>Being motivated</u>** – become a "self-starter"; be open to learning new ways of achievement

- **<u>Trying to understand people</u>** – being a "team member" is vital; develop compassion and wisdom when dealing with others

- **<u>Being willing to work</u>** – in order to achieve, you must be willing to work many long, hard hours . . . as an individual as well as working with others

Good luck to you as you prepare for your future. Continue to be optimistic. Remember, as you stated, "nothing ventured, nothing gained".

Sincerely,

Edward E. Crutchfield

Edward E. Crutchfield

"BEING A TEAM MEMBER IS VITAL; DEVELOP COMPASSION AND WISDOM WHEN DEALING WITH OTHERS."

—EDWARD E. CRUTCHFIELD, Chairman and CEO, First Union National Bank (now Wachovia), Charlotte, NC

"You have to also know how to get the support of other people and have them want to see you succeed. If people 'do not wish you well' you will have great difficulty."

—JUDITH M. VON SELDENECK, CHAIRMAN, THE DIVERSIFIED SEARCH COMPANIES, PHILADELPHIA, PA

"MY PATH CAME OVER TIME; IT WAS NOT AN EPIPHANY OR REVELATION. IT WAS A SLOW MATURING AS A LEADER, REALIZING THAT PEOPLE RESPOND BEST TO THOSE THAT TREAT THEM WITH DIGNITY AND RESPECT RATHER THAN BY 'COMMAND AND CONTROL.'"

—JAMES H. BLANCHARD, Chairman and CEO, Synovus, Columbus, GA

Carlos M. Gutierrez
President
Chief Executive Officer

January 10, 2000

Mr. Douglas Barry

Voorhees, New Jersey 08043

Dear Doug:

This is in response to your January 3 letter asking about the qualities that contributed to my success. I consider it an honor to be asked, and I hope my comments will be helpful.

I strongly believe that one should plan for the qualities you want to develop in yourself. Hard work, along with honesty, respect, and confidence, make up a strong plan for success. You may see others who seem to get things "the easy way" for a while, but that kind of success is often short-lived. Giving honest value for whatever job you do earns the respect of the people you work for, the people you work with, and later, the people who work for you. Their respect helps to build your confidence. When you are confident about your ability to be the best, you gain the support of others who will help you succeed and stay successful.

I have always been an "inspired" Kellogg employee trying to optimize my abilities toward doing the very best that I could for this company. While "self-inspiration" certainly helps, it isn't enough to propel anyone into a leadership position. Your fellow employees need to believe that you are the best person for leadership and that you are the person that they want to willingly follow. What gains the support of your fellow employees is hard work, fairness, good listening ability, courage, and being right on the issues.

It has been my experience at Kellogg Company that success creates more success. I have been very lucky to have opportunities to build each accomplishment into a bigger one. The traits I chose to develop (hard work, honesty, respect for myself and others, and confidence) have carried me through many challenges in my career. I can truthfully say that I wouldn't trade any of those challenges or qualities for the chance to have it all "the easy way."

Douglas, I hope my comments are helpful in your own plan for success. My best wishes to you for the future. . .it looks like you have a great start!

Sincerely,

Carlos M. Gutierrez
President
Chief Executive Officer

"I believe in treating other people with respect. My style is to speak to people, be available to them and willing to answer their questions. This also means being straightforward and honest with them."

—**SANFORD I. WEILL**, CHAIRMAN AND CO-CEO, CITIGROUP, INC., NEW YORK, NY

"You may be tough but you must be absolutely fair with all employees."

—WALLACE D. MALONE JR., CEO, SouthTrust Corp., Birmingham, AL

"LEADERS ARE MOST EFFECTIVE WHEN THEY MAKE EVERYONE WHO WORKS FOR THEM FEEL VALUED. THAT IS WHY FORWARD-THINKING BUSINESSES NOW PUT A PREMIUM ON CREATING AN ENVIRONMENT THAT ENCOURAGES EMPLOYEES TO SHARE IDEAS, ANALYSES, OR ADVICE THAT LEAD TO SUCCESSFUL OUTCOMES."

—JUDITH RODIN, President, University of Pennsylvania, Philadelphia, PA

Inspiration Gets Reply

Q: What are the qualities that best prepared you for becoming a CEO?

A: "Being highly competitive, but always playing fair and caring deeply about your teammates. Understanding who my customers are, what they like most about my brand, and then working very hard to give them more of what they like. Deploying my communications skills to energize everyone toward a vision—as you energized me to take the time and write back to you."

—LEONARD H. ROBERTS, CEO,
RADIO SHACK CORPORATION, FORTH WORTH, TX

"THERE IS NOTHING WORSE IN A JOB ENVIRONMENT THAN A BULLYING BOSS."

—JACK O. BOVENDER JR., Chairman and CEO, HCA, Nashville, TN

"The best way to have others join in supporting your goals is to care about them as people and demonstrate your respect for them. We like to say that 'Love is a better motivator than fear.'"

—REUBEN MARK, CHAIRMAN AND CEO, COLGATE-PALMOLIVE CO., NEW YORK, NY

"ALWAYS TREAT PEOPLE WITH DIGNITY AND RESPECT, PARTICULARLY THOSE WHO WORK FOR YOU. NOT ONLY IS THIS APPROPRIATE BEHAVIOR— IF YOU FOLLOW THIS PRINCIPLE, YOU WILL ATTRACT AND RETAIN TALENTED PEOPLE, WHICH YOU WILL FIND IS ESSENTIAL TO YOUR SUCCESS."

—RAYMOND V. GILMARTIN, Chairman, President and CEO, Merck & Co., Whitehouse Station, NJ

Lawrence A. Weinbach
Chairman, President, and
Chief Executive Officer

Unisys Corporation
PO Box 500
Blue Bell PA 19424 0001

UNISYS

February 22, 2000

Mr. Douglas Barry

Voorhees, NJ 08043

Dear Douglas:

Thank you for your letter asking me about what I believe to be important qualities that prepared me to become a CEO.

First, I think that one of the most important qualities is being a good listener. I try to give the person I am speaking with my full and direct attention, and to really focus on what they are saying. Too often we can miss important and valuable messages that others are sending us by not giving them the attention they deserve.

The second quality that comes to mind is self-confidence, or more precisely "desirable" self-confidence. By this I mean that it is important that others can clearly see that you are confident in your leadership role. The "desirable" part may sound a bit unusual. Self-confidence can sometimes get out of hand and become "self-importance." This is not a quality that I think serves a CEO well.

A third important quality for a CEO is being someone people can trust. As chief executive officer of a public company, you are responsible to shareholders for the care and growth of the organization's assets, and just as important, for the people who are your fellow employees. I have always believed that people are the most important part of any organization, and to lead people successfully they need to trust you and your commitment to them and to the organization as a whole.

I hope these thoughts will help you with your project. I have enclosed a copy of the Unisys Annual Report for 1998 (the 1999 report is being printed). This report will help if you wish to learn more about Unisys.

Thanks again for your letter.

Sincerely,

Lawrence A. Weinbach

ss
Enclosure

Charles M. Cawley
Chairman and
Chief Executive Officer

March 6, 2000

MBNA America Bank, N.A.
Wilmington, Delaware 19884-0141

Mr. Douglas Barry

Voorhees, NJ 08043

Dear Douglas:

I am responding to the note you sent me a few weeks ago. I am honored to be among those you are consulting, and I commend your initiative. With such a clear goal in mind already, I'm sure you'll make a fine corporate executive some day.

To reach that goal, keep in mind a few things I've learned and practiced in the years I've been a manager and a CEO. First, the people of your company do not work for you — you work for them. They are the people who make your product, sell it to buyers, and take care of your Customers. Use your position to create an atmosphere in which they enjoy working and they will use all of their talents to satisfy the Customer.

Second, reward excellence. Work with your colleagues to set clear goals for your company, communicate those goals to the people working there, and acknowledge and congratulate the people who achieve and exceed their goals. They'll be more inclined to do so again, and their co-workers will find inspiration in their friends' recognition.

Third, listen. Leadership has less to do with walking in front and leading the way than it does with listening to the needs of the people of the company and meeting them. Stay in touch with your co-workers and encourage them to stay in touch with you to make sure you are all working together to satisfy Customers and grow your business.

The last tip I offer is one you seem to have demonstrated already: Be confident in yourself and your abilities. Leaders are often models to those they lead. They lead by example, not by words. Your self-confidence will inspire it in others. But as I said, I don't think you'll have any problems there.

I hope these are helpful, Douglas, and I wish you continued success in school and beyond. If you can develop these qualities, follow these steps, and continue to consult those who've gone before you, I'm sure you'll achieve your goal.

Sincerely,

Charles Jackson

"You need to learn to deal with people! . . . from the janitor to the Chairman."

—DAVID PERDUE, Chairman and CEO, Dollar General, Goodlettsville, TN

"ONE OF THE MOST IMPORTANT QUALITIES [OF A CEO] IS BEING A GOOD LISTENER. I TRY TO GIVE THE PERSON I AM SPEAKING WITH MY FULL ATTENTION, AND TO REALLY FOCUS ON WHAT THEY ARE SAYING. TOO OFTEN WE CAN MISS IMPORTANT AND VALUABLE MESSAGES THAT OTHERS ARE SENDING US BY NOT GIVING THEM THE ATTENTION THEY DESERVE."

—LAWRENCE A. WEINBACH, Chairman, President, and CEO, Unisys, Blue Bell, PA

"THE PEOPLE OF YOUR COMPANY DO NOT WORK FOR YOU—YOU WORK FOR THEM."

—CHARLES M. CAWLEY, Chairman and CEO, MBNA America, Wilmington, DE

"First, treat people right and fairly. Give people the tools they need to do the job and the authority to use them. They will generally surprise you."

—J. KENNETH GLASS, PRESIDENT AND CEO, FIRST TENNESSEE BANK, MEMPHIS, TN

"The only CEO that walks on water is one that has a talented team of executives holding their breath under the water in order to hold him/her up."

—JACK M. GREENBERG, chairman and CEO, McDonald's Corp., Oak Brook, IL

"THE POSSIBILITY OF SUCCESS ALWAYS LIES WITHIN YOUR PEOPLE. ALL THE BEST INVESTMENTS, STRATEGIES AND TACTICS WILL FAIL WITHOUT THEIR BUY-IN AND ENERGY. COMMUNICATE WITH THEM, SEEK OUT THEIR IDEAS, IMPLEMENT THEM."

—LARRY JOHNSON, CEO, Albertsons Inc., Boise, ID

Jack M. Greenberg
Chairman & CEO

February 4, 2000

Mr. Douglas Barry

Voorhees, NJ 08043

Dear Mr. Barry:

Thank you for your letter and for sharing your career aspirations with me.

I have found that the two best qualities a CEO can have are the ability to listen and to assume the best motives in others. I am the first person to admit that I don't know the answer to every problem. I look to every person who works at McDonald's, from the restaurant crew member to my peers, to help me make the best decisions for our company.

After all, it isn't often that a company's success is determined by one person. As you continue towards your career goals, remember the following: the only CEO that walks on water is one that has a talented team of executives holding their breath under the water in order to hold him/her up.

I appreciate your support and wish you much success in life.

Regards,

Jack M. Greenberg

Jack M. Greenberg

QuikTrip. Corporation

CORPORATE OFFICE
4705 South 129th East Avenue
Tulsa, Oklahoma 74134-7008
P.O. Box 3475
Tulsa, Oklahoma 74101-3475

QT

May 5, 2003

Mr. Douglas Barry

Voorhees, NJ 08043

Dear Doug:

It is obvious that you have the intellect and the desire to be a successful CEO. What I don't know is if you have the guts and the heart. You understand guts, but being successful also means really caring about people and making sure they are successful too.

Best wishes,

Chester Cadieux
Chairman of the Board

What I've Learned

I always had the impression that "the boss" was someone to be respected and feared, because if you get "the boss" upset, you'll lose your job.

Respect, I believed, was mostly reserved for and given to the person in charge. I also thought respect in the workplace was a one-way street, with all of it going in the boss's direction and none coming back toward the employees. But I have learned through these letters that, in order to get people motivated to reach for individual goals and to share in an overall vision, the leader has to give respect to others in order to receive it back from them. Only by being conscious of employees' needs and challenges, and serving them, will the leader in turn earn their people's respect.

Also, as these letters echo again and again, it's clear that it is the average workers and not the higher-up executives that make an organization prosper or fail. The leader who does not recognize this fact is in for a tough time.

Mr. Jack Greenberg offered an interesting spin on the leadership position that resonated with me. He used an interesting metaphor to explain how a leader's visible accomplishments are only possible with the behind-the-scenes support of his or her team. And he made it clear that these "invisible" team heroics can only be expected when the leader is well-respected. As all successful CEOs will tell you, a well-respected leader becomes such in only one way: by earning it. In other words, if you are able to respect and treat people as individuals and get them to respect you, then they will do amazing things for you, and for themselves.

Vision

CLEARLY COMMUNICATE THE FUTURE

vi.sion (noun):
intelligent foresight
—American Heritage Dictionary, 3rd Edition

"To have big success, you must have big dreams, and you must be willing to take a chance."

—SUMNER M. REDSTONE, CHAIRMAN AND CEO, VIACOM INC., NEW YORK, NY

Leaders do not need to be visionaries—those who can see into and predict the future. But they do have to have a vision—a plan for the future prosperity and ultimate destiny of their company. The greatest lesson learned about vision from today's leaders is that a vision can't come into focus without involving others. (After all, did you ever have a dream that involved only you? If you did, it was probably a nightmare). "Vision," "dream," "risk," and "chance," I found, are words CEOs tend to use quite often, and often in the same sentence speaking of the same goal. Another word they use when speaking in these terms, is "we."

On Vision:

To believe your own thought, to believe that what is true for you in your private heart is true for all men—that is genius. Speak your latent conviction, and it shall be the universal sense; for the inmost in due time becomes the outmost, and our first thought is rendered back to us by the trumpets of the Last Judgment. Familiar as the voice of the mind is to each, the highest merit we ascribe to Moses, Plato, and Milton is that they set at naught books and traditions, and spoke not what men, but what they thought. A man should learn to detect and watch that gleam of light which flashes across his mind from within, more than the lustre of the firmament of bards and sages. Yet he dismisses without notice his thought, because it is his. In every work of genius we recognize our own rejected thoughts; they come back to us with a certain alienated majesty. Great works of art have no more affecting lesson for us than this. They teach us to abide by our spontaneous impression with good-humored inflexibility than most when the whole cry of voices is on the other side. Else to-morrow a stranger will say with masterly good sense precisely what we have thought and felt all the time, and we shall be forced to take with shame our own opinion from another.

There is a time in every man's education when he arrives at the conviction that envy is ignorance; that imitation is suicide; that he must take himself for better for worse as his portion; that though the wide universe is full of good, no kernel of nourishing corn can come to him but through his toil bestowed on that plot of ground which is given to him to till. The power which resides in him is new in nature, and none but he knows what that is which he can do, nor does he know until he has tried. . . . A man is relieved and gay when he has put his heart into his work and done his best; but what he has said or done otherwise shall give him no peace.

—RALPH WALDO EMERSON,
FROM *SELF-RELIANCE*

"THE BEST CEOS BUILD THE TEAM TO ACHIEVE THE DREAM."

—CHARLES R. LEE, Chairman and CEO, GTE Corp., Irving, TX

"LEADERSHIP REQUIRES, AT TIMES, THE WILLINGNESS TO EXPLORE IDEAS AND CONCEPTS BEYOND THE TRADITIONAL WAYS WE HAVE ALWAYS MANAGED; THE WILLINGNESS TO TAKE CHANCES, TO FAIL, AND TO GO RIGHT BACK AND TRY AGAIN."

—CORBIN A. MCNEILL JR., President, Chairman and CEO, PECO Energy, Philadelphia, PA

"One of the key qualities that any CEO (or successful person) needs—a willingness to stretch yourself and go after goals that others think are too visionary, too hard, or too ambitious to accomplish."

—RICHARD A. MCGINN, CHAIRMAN AND CEO, LUCENT TECHNOLOGIES, MURRAY HILL, NJ

Lucent Technologies
Bell Labs Innovations

Richard A. McGinn   600 Mountain Avenue
Chairman and   Murray Hill, NJ 07974
Chief Executive Officer

January 19, 2000

Douglas Barry

Vorhees, New Jersey 08043

Dear Douglas,

I think that you have already hit on one of the key qualities that any CEO (or successful person) needs – a willingness to stretch yourself and go after goals that others think are too visionary, too hard, or too ambitious to accomplish. I've found that a healthy dose of audacity and a willingness to take chances have always served me well. Just as important, however, is the ability to listen and learn from the people around you – to have an open mind that responds to the quality of an idea without stumbling over preconceptions based on *who* is putting it forth. As a leader, I'm willing to take chances, but I have the responsibility to make sure that they are not reckless ones. I constantly work to put together a diverse business team that brings different experiences and points of view to bear on the opportunities and challenges we face on a daily basis.

Hope that these quick thoughts help you. Good luck on whatever directions you head towards (and I'm sure there will be several) as you move through your life.

Best regards,

Rich Mc Ginn

Georgia-Pacific Corporation

133 Peachtree Street, N.E.
P.O. Box 105605
Atlanta, Georgia 30348

A.D. Correll
Chairman of the Board and
Chief Executive Officer

February 22, 2000

Douglas Barry

Vorhees, New Jersey 08043

Dear Douglas:

I admire you for taking the initiative to think about your future at such an early age. You obviously are a bright young man who already has many of the qualities that are required to succeed in business.

As to the question of what qualities helped me succeed, I attribute my success to two key things: 1) always doing a job to the best of my abilities regardless of the time necessary to do so, and 2) a willingness to take some risks along the way.

I learned early in my career that I could accomplish more in a 60-hour- week than most people could accomplish in a 40-hour-week. That's the humorous way I explain my willingness to work hard to do the best job I can, no matter what the task.

As a young man about your age, I learned the value and necessity of hard work by helping my mother run our family clothing store in Brunswick, Ga. The nice thing about running a small store was that success was easily measured. If there was more money in the cash drawer at the end of the day than at the beginning, you had a successful day.

As for taking risks, I often tell the story of how I worked as a clothing salesman for J.C. Penney after completing college, but ultimately decided that it was not my long-range career ambition. So, I took a risk and went to work in a business that I knew nothing about – papermaking. That decision changed my entire life.

I hope this answers your question. I wish you the best of luck in school and in your pursuit to succeed in business.

Sincerely,

"NO ONE GETS TO THE TOP BY HIMSELF OR HERSELF."

—JAMES M. ZIMMERMAN, Chairman and CEO, Federated Department Stores Inc., Cincinnati, OH

"THE PEOPLE YOU LEAD WANT TO KNOW WHERE THEY ARE GOING. YOU NEED TO COMMUNICATE A VISION THAT IS CLEAR, COMPELLING, CREDIBLE, CHALLENGING AND WORTH THE EFFORT. THE HARDEST PART IS DEVELOPING A VISION TO SHARE."

—CHRISTOPHER B. GALVIN, Chairman and CEO, Motorola, Inc., Schaumburg, IL

"Success is for those who know what they want and go after it, no matter how difficult the path."

—JACQUES A. NASSER, President and CEO, Ford Motor Company, Dearborn, MI

"SHARE THE VISION. IT'S IMPORTANT TO DEVELOP A SENSE OF SHARED DESTINY IN PEOPLE. A VISION CANNOT BELONG TO JUST ONE LEADER— OTHER PEOPLE HAVE TO OWN IT, TOO."

—JAMES H. BLANCHARD, Chairman and CEO, Synovus, Columbus, GA

Share the Vision

"Whether you consider the success or failings of a company, a country, or even a religion, the outcomes are all driven by its people—people as individuals and people as teams. A great leader understands that to lead you must know what it is like to follow. To create a vision for people to pursue, you must be better than a good communicator—you must be an extraordinary translator of dreams, a demonstrator of passion for pursuing the dream, and a proven believer that it is your people who can and will deliver the dream. And then, you start all over again."

—ROSEMARIE B. GRECO,
DIRECTOR, OFFICE OF HEALTH CARE REFORM,
HARRISBURG, PA

"A leader's job is to clarify and simplify so that everyone understands what's truly important. Express your ideas in terms everyone can grasp. No one can follow a road map they can't read."

—REUBEN MARK, CHAIRMAN AND CEO,
COLGATE-PALMOLIVE CO., NEW YORK, NY

"I learned to lead by figuring out how to get other people to buy into my idea and expand on it through their own intelligence and drive."

—MICHAEL H. JORDAN, CEO, Electronic Data Systems, Plano, TX

"THE SKILLS THAT PERMIT A PERSON TO BE A SUCCESSFUL CEO, IN MY OPINION, ARE: BEING A STRATEGIC VISIONARY, A GOOD COMMUNICATOR [AND] A BUILDER OF COMPETENT TEAMS."

—R. KEITH ELLIOTT, Chairman, Hercules Inc., Wilmington, DE

▮HERCULES

Hercules Incorporated
Hercules Plaza
1313 North Market Street
Wilmington, DE 19894-0001

January 10, 2000

Mr. Douglas Barry

Voorhees, NJ 08043

R. Keith Elliott
Chairman of the Board

Dear Mr. Barry:

Your letter of January 3, 2000 was interesting, intriguing and has had me thinking for a few days. There are several levels on which I could answer the question but that would only complicate what was a simple question that deserves a rather simple answer.

If you don't mind, I am going to analyze the question in this letter and let you read what my thought process was in getting to the answer, and that way you can argue with the logic or not. First, the single best lesson that I ever learned in business and the thing that made everything else possible in my business life was learned in my very first job at DuPont and was passed on to me by my second supervisor. He, by the way, became a very successful fellow in the DuPont financial organization. It was simple but it never, but never, failed to produce results. He said "don't concentrate on the end goal but rather do the very best job that you can in the job you are in and others will always want you to work for them". If you behave this way, you can experience varied situations in business and will be exposed to things that you might never imagine. As you get older and are competing for higher and higher levels of responsibility in a major corporation, those that usually get the job are those with the broadest and best experience that have performed at the highest levels in many different kinds of situations.

Being chosen to be the CEO of a major company is a rare thing indeed. Some of the things that have to be in place for that to happen are: 1) one must have a gift of intelligence but have also cultivated that gift over the years; 2) one has to be lucky regarding being at the right company, in the right job and at the right time to assume that role; 3) one must have self confidence but be humble enough to realize that true success is the ability to harness the best ideas of the team; 4) one must have demonstrated an ability to make sound decisions over an extended period of time and in an appropriate variety of situations; and 5) one must have gained the confidence of the CEO's boss, the board of directors.

Some truisms that I have learned by being the CEO of a large multi-national manufacturing company are: a) no one, but no one ever tells you the complete truth that is free of any bias—lots of people try to, but even the best intentioned person has some sort of agenda and tilts the data—others actually lie or fail to tell all they know about a situation so that the outcome is the way they hope; b) multiple opinions on every major subject is crucial for the CEO to get the full picture; c) loneliness is a key ingredient of the job—when the decision works out well, you will have plenty of folks who say they supported the idea; when it does not, no one can be found. However, while the jury is still out on the outcome of the decision, there are numerous fence sitters who can go either way. In the end, the CEO must get advice from his key advisors on every major decision, never decide until you have both the positives and negatives clearly understood and then go with your "gut" about what to do.

While the job has its bad moments and creates a huge amount of stress in the incumbent, it is also the best job I ever had. Being ultimately responsible for the performance of a major company and all its employees is the highest high there is and was worth all the years of preparation and sacrifice. After saying that I would not answer you on two levels, I have decided to do so anyway. First, I will answer the question that you asked, "what are the two or three qualities that best prepared you to become CEO" and secondly, I am going to attempt the two or three skills that permit a person to be successful as a CEO. In both cases, the model is a large multi-national manufacturing company. I say that because the answers may be different if the company was a large retailer, for example.

The qualities that best prepared me to become a CEO, in my opinion, are:
1. Constant pursuit of excellence
2. Ability to listen
3. Willingness to take risks

The skills that permit a person to be a successful CEO, in my opinion, are:
1. Being a strategic visionary
2. A good communicator
3. A builder of competent teams

Douglas, it has been fun to think through this letter and I hope you find it useful. While it is good to have goals as a young adult, it is even more important to enjoy your time as a young man. Don't clutter it up with too many grown up goals and ideals. There will be plenty of time to do all those great things. You are very fortunate to have the family that you do. I know both your mom and dad and like them both very much. I have never worked with your dad but have done so with your mom. She is very good at what she does and has obviously been a great mom to you if you want to emulate her career.

Best wishes and good luck to you.

Very truly yours,

Keith Elliott
Chairman of the Board

cc: J. B. Barry

Christopher B. Galvin

Chairman of the Board and
Chief Executive Officer

February 3, 2000

Douglas Barry

Voorhees, New Jersey 08043

Dear Douglas:

Thank you for your letter concerning two or three qualities of business leadership for CEOs. I'll mention three, and they all begin with E.

The first is <u>envisioning</u>. The people you lead want to know where they are going. You need to communicate a vision that is clear, compelling, credible, challenging and worth the effort. The hardest part is developing a vision to share. It means you keep up with the latest changes in your industry and the world. You need to listen to your customers and to the people who are closest to those customers.

The second is <u>energizing</u>. When you demonstrate your own personal excitement and energy, you motivate the people around you to share that spirit and energy. The best motivator of all, of course, is success. The ability to lead your team to victory generates the kind of energy that can drive continued success.

The third is <u>enabling</u>. The leader needs to create the environment that enables their teams to succeed. It requires the right tools and the right training. For example, Motorola is leading the way to an age in which individuals and work groups stay in touch through wireless Internet technology. That's transforming the way we live and work. Our people need a tremendous amount of knowledge and education to stay at the edge of this change. What you learn in school is just the beginning. A leader needs to enable creative people to achieve breakthroughs at the cutting edge.

Those are three good qualities of leadership, but there's another word that begins with E that is absolutely essential. That word is <u>ethics</u>. Leadership means nothing unless you adhere to the highest standards of ethical behavior. That means treating all people with dignity and respect, and acting with uncompromising integrity in everything you do.

Good luck with your project. You're on your way to becoming a great leader.

Regards,

Chris Galvin

"AT VARIOUS POINTS IN YOUR CAREERS, YOU WILL BE CALLED TO TAKE A RISK. AND I THINK YOU WILL FIND, AS I HAVE FOUND, THOSE WILL BE THE TIMES OF YOUR GREATEST OPPORTUNITIES."

—RAYMOND V. GILMARTIN, Chairman, President and CEO, Merck & Co., Whitehouse Station, NJ

"Learn to understand and trust your head and your heart. Intuition cannot be learned in books and that takes time."

—RAY ELLIOT, CHAIRMAN, PRESIDENT AND CEO, ZIMMER HOLDINGS INC.

"THERE WAS NO SINGLE TURNING POINT FOR ME IN BECOMING A LEADER, BUT A GRADUAL RECOGNITION THAT I COULD HAVE AN INFLUENCE ON THE DIRECTION OF AN ORGANIZATION OR A PROJECT IF I STEPPED FORWARD AND TOOK RESPONSIBILITY."

—SHARON A. SMITH, CEO, Girl Scouts of Southeastern Pennsylvania, Miquon, PA

"A business leader knows how to distinguish between what is vital and what is merely desirable."

—WILLIAM C. STEERE JR., Chairman and CEO, Pfizer, Inc., New York, NY

"As a leader, you must have a vision or a goal. Make a vision that's yours, and that others will want to follow."

—PAT CROCE, FORMER PRESIDENT, PHILADELPHIA 76ERS, PHILADELPHIA, PA

"FAILURE OFTEN RESULTS WHEN LEADERS DO NOT COMMUNICATE CLEARLY IN LANGUAGE UNDERSTOOD BY THEIR AUDIENCE, AND THEY ARE CERTAIN TO FAIL IF THEY IGNORE INPUT FROM COLLEAGUES AND DIRECT REPORTS."

—H.A. WAGNER, Chairman and CEO, Air Products and Chemicals Inc., Allentown, PA

Set Priorities

"My ability to prioritize has proven beneficial in focusing both personal time and energy as well as that of the corporation. The ability to prioritize further helps set forth strategic direction of a company and assists in communicating to those involved just what is important for the success of those goals."

—HOWARD E. COSGROVE,
CEO, CONECTIV, WILMINGTON, DE

Share the Glory

"You'll never succeed alone. You must surround yourself with a diverse group of motivated, talented, energetic people. You must send a clear vision, ensure everyone understands that vision and what their role is in helping achieve that vision. Then you've got to stay on top of their progress, keep them focused on the vision and the actions that must be undertaken to achieve it, then praise, coach and work with them every step of the way. That's the nature of leadership, and it requires the ability to assess people and to motivate them to action."

—CHARLES MORGAN, Chairman,
Acxiom Corporation, Little Rock, AK

William C. Steere, Jr.
Chairman of the Board and
Chief Executive Officer

February 7, 2000

Mr. Douglas Barry

Voorhees, NJ 08043

Dear Douglas:

Thank you very much for your letter. I am delighted to know that you are
studying leadership in school, and that you have set high goals for yourself.

There are many factors that account for success in the business world. But in my
experience, the most important of them is focus. A business leader knows how to
distinguish between what is vital and what is merely desirable. He or she sets
ambitious but attainable goals, and ensures that others in the organization have the
resources and motivation they need to work together to achieve those goals.

At Pfizer, throughout the 1990s we've focused on our core mission of discovering,
developing, and bringing to market innovative medicines that enable humans and
animals to live longer and healthier lives. We've gotten out of several lines of
business that, although good in themselves, did not fit with our core competencies.
I'm convinced that focusing on what we do best has been instrumental in making
Pfizer the number-one pharmaceutical company in the world.

Thank you again for writing. I wish you every success in setting – and achieving –
your own goals.

Sincerely,

William C. Steere, Jr.

Viacom Inc.
1515 Broadway
New York NY 10036-5794

Sumner M. Redstone
Chairman of the Board and
Chief Executive Officer

February 2, 2000

Mr. Douglas Barry

Voorhees, NJ 08043

Dear Mr. Barry:

Thank you for writing. I am always delighted to hear from young people like yourself.

My experience has taught me that the three qualities a successful CEO must possess are: a passionate commitment to your goal; the courage to dream and to take risks; and the moral and intellectual character to realize the dreams worth pursuing and the best route to take to achieve them.

To have big successes, you must have big dreams, and you must be willing to take a chance. You must also realize that all your hard work in school will be worth it. If you take what you learn in school and add passion, dedication, and a will to win, there are no limits to what you can accomplish.

Thanks again for thinking of me and best of luck.

Sincerely,

Sumner M. Redstone

A Grandfather's Vision

Q: Was there a turning point in your career that brought you down the path to become the leader you are today?

A: The turning point for me took place on the day I graduated from high school. I had not planned to go to college. My parents were first generation immigrants without a high school education. No relatives ever went to college. My grandfather came up, with tears in his eyes, gave me a hug and an envelope. It contained a few hundred dollars. He said he came to America to create a better life for his family and I was the first with the ability to attend college. He taught me a lesson about responsibility, and the rest is history.

—JON A. BOSCIA, Chairman and CEO,
Lincoln Financial Group, Philadelphia, PA

What I've Learned

We are propelled forward by our dreams, and it's obvious through my correspondence with CEOs that a good leader always offers a clear vision for his or her organization that is both attainable and inspiring.

M r. Jordan, in fact, shared how he learned to be a leader "by figuring out how to get other people to buy into my idea and expand on it…"

Many of the letters I received suggested the simple but important notion that in order to accomplish something, you have to know how you're going to go about accomplishing it. I started lifting weights towards the end of my sophomore year. I didn't have a plan, really, except that I wanted to get bigger. And I soon discovered that it was difficult to keep going every day. But I remembered that in order to accomplish my ultimate goal, I had to set out a specific plan and to start accomplishing smaller, more attainable goals along the way—even when many of those little goals were extremely strenuous. I also remembered what Mr. Jacques Nasser wrote to me: that successful people go after what they want "no matter how difficult the path."

Everyone has goals and dreams, but not everyone follows through with their plans consistently. How many broken New Year's resolutions have you had? How many times have you failed to fulfill a commitment? It's clear that in order to succeed and to lead, you have to set out on a definite course of action. And not only must you motivate yourself, but to be a good leader, you have to motivate everyone around you and inspire in them a confidence in your vision and your will to succeed. Mr. Croce of the Philadelphia 76ers put it best when he told me to "create a unique vision, one that others will want to follow."

I tried to put those words into action right away. Making this book was a vision of mine, and, as I began to put my ideas into motion, I inspired my parents and my friends to help me along the way.

Humanity

IT'S NOT JUST ABOUT THE PAYCHECK

hu.mane **(adjective):**
marked by an emphasis on
humanistic values and concerns.
—American Heritage Dictionary, 3rd Edition

"The bottom line about success in life isn't whether you are financially successful, but whether you have given of yourself in some way to help others less fortunate than you and to serve your community and your country."

—P. ANTHONY RIDDER, CHAIRMAN AND CEO, KNIGHT RIDDER, SAN JOSE, CA

T rue leaders do not wear rose-colored glasses, earplugs, or blinders. They are capable of listening to issues that others experience and seeing the world as others see it. More importantly, they are willing to be part of their community and help make it a better place in which to live. Great CEOs, I've learned, embrace cultural diversity, go beyond the confines of their own little world in pursuit of bigger ideas, and foster an environment that allows others to prosper. And they seem to do so for just the right reason: because it is the right thing to do.

On Humanity:

Great part of that order which reigns among mankind is not the effect of Government. It has its origin in the principles of society and the natural constitution of man. It existed prior to Government, and would exist if the formality of Government was abolished. The mutual dependence and reciprocal interest which man has upon man, and all the parts of a civilised community upon each other, create that great chain of connection which holds it together. The landholder, the farmer, the manufacturer, the merchant, the tradesman, and every occupation, prospers by the aid which each receives from the other, and from the whole. Common interest regulates their concerns, and forms their law; and the laws which common usage ordains, have a greater influence than the laws of Government. In fine, society performs for itself almost everything which is ascribed to Government.

To understand the nature and quantity of Government proper for man, it is necessary to attend to his character. As nature created him for social life, she fitted him for the station she intended. In all cases she made his natural wants greater than his individual powers. No one man is capable, without the aid of society, of supplying his own wants;

and those wants, acting upon every individual, impel the whole of them into society, as naturally as gravitation acts to a centre.

But she has gone further. She has not only forced man into society by a diversity of wants which the reciprocal aid of each other can supply, but she has implanted in him a system of social affections, which, though not necessary to his existence, are essential to his happiness. There is no period in life when this love for society ceases to act. It begins and ends with our being.

If we examine with attention the composition and constitution of man, the diversity of his wants and talents in different men for reciprocally accommodating the wants of each other, his propensity to society, and consequently to preserve the advantages resulting from it, we shall easily discover that a great part of what is called Government is mere imposition.

Government is no farther necessary than to supply the few cases to which society and civilisation are not conveniently competent; and instances are not wanting to show, that everything which Government can usefully add thereto, has been performed by the common consent of society, without Government.

—THOMAS PAINE, FROM *RIGHTS OF MAN*

American Water Works Company, Inc.

1025 Laurel Oak Road • P.O. Box 1770 • Voorhees, New Jersey 08043
Executive Assistant: Linda K. Stuffle

Marilyn Ware
Chairman of the Board

February 10, 2000

Douglas Barry

Voorhees, NJ 08043

Dear Douglas,

Thank you for your letter of January 14th and the interesting questions which you posed in it. I am pleased to respond. However, I think my response can be the most help if it deviates a slight bit from the actual questions.

Your resume was an interesting one and your background seems to present ideal opportunities to prepare you to be a CEO **and also** a civic leader. I think the two are inextricably linked as real leadership is seldom containable. Leaders are drawn to finding more than one way to benefit this wonderful society in which we live. Certainly creating and sustaining jobs is important. Although I am the Chairman of our Board and not the CEO, I feel an immense responsibility to both our shareholders and our employees. As Chairman, I feel that the ultimate responsibility for providing beneficial direction for both groups rests on my shoulders.

Beyond that I know that my position gives me a platform to improve our society in several indirect ways — that is by supporting important charities and talented individuals who are changing our world for the better. Having a father who is a doctor, and a mother who is an executive, must allow you to see the best of several worlds through the eyes of two people you love. Yes, medicine is a business but it is also about people; and business executives are primarily occupied with *business* but want to create a better world in other ways as well.

These comments may appear unrelated to the direct approach which you sought in posing your questions. I hope they are one way of reminding you, observe your parents to see the qualities which they posses. For instance, I think you will observe that they take well-reasoned risks.

My grandfather helped prepare me to become a leader. He was a demanding yet loving mentor who always reminded me that I had the talent to become anything that I chose. This eventually became my own theme and his sense of adventure (and encouragement) inspired me to set my own goals. I never even considered that they might be unrealistically high. Here I am, years later, chairman of this fine company after first having raised a family of three wonderful children and I always believed that I would succeed at both.

Along those same lines, please don't believe people when they say CEOs are too busy to answer questions "from school kids." There is nothing demeaning or inferior about being young — it is simply a statement of chronology. There is certainly nothing inferior about being in school — it is a treasured place where I sometimes wish I could be. As an adult, I am bombarded with choices and the ways to implement them, but too seldom have the opportunity to immerse myself deeply in traditional learning. I hope you will always feel the pure joy of learning and being taught.

Please send me the final copy of your class project and, if you choose, your report cards so far. I would like to see the strengths which such an interesting young man possesses. Are you a shareholder?

Best wishes,

"A LEADER SEEKS AND CULTIVATES DIVERSITY . . . DIVERSITY OF IDEAS, STYLE, CULTURE, GENDER, AND RACE. LEADERS KNOW THAT IDEAS ARE WHAT COUNTS, AND THAT THEY COME FROM ALL OVER."

—WILLIAM STAVROPOULOS, President and CEO, Dow Chemical Co., Midland, MI

"One must understand how their actions impact not only their particular job, but the functioning of the organization as a whole. This is something like being able to see both the forest and the trees."

—PHILIP J. CARROLL, CHAIRMAN AND CEO, FLUOR CORP., ALISO VIEJO, CA

"BELIEVE IN PEOPLE. THE FURTHER ONE GOES IN LIFE, THE MORE HIS/HER ACCOMPLISHMENTS DEPEND ON OTHER PEOPLE. CREATE AN ENVIRONMENT IN WHICH EVERYONE CAN CONTRIBUTE AND WHERE DIVERSITY IN ALL ITS DIMENSIONS PROSPERS."

—GEORGE M.C. FISHER, Chairman of the Board, Eastman Kodak Co., Rochester, NY

William S. Stavropoulos
President and Chief Executive Officer

The Dow Chemical Company
2030 Dow Center
Midland, Michigan 48674-2030

March 19, 2000

Douglas Barry

Voorhees, New Jersey 08043

Dear Douglas,

I'm happy to share with you my thoughts on becoming a CEO. In fact, you've already adopted one trait I think is very important, which is that a leader recognizes risk is always the companion of opportunity. Leaders aren't afraid of failure and encourage others to try new ideas.

Second, a leader seeks and cultivates diversity ... diversity of ideas, style, culture, gender, and race. Leaders know that <u>ideas are what counts,</u> and that they come from all over.

The most successful people I see are those that are able to preserve their core beliefs while at the same time strive to stay in front of an ever-changing world. Dwight Eisenhower once said that "Leadership is action, not position." My best wishes to you Douglas.

William Stavropoulos

 **Progress Energy**

William Cavanaugh III
Chairman and Chief Executive Officer

July 16, 2003

Mr. Douglas Barry

Voorhees, NJ 08043

Dear Mr. Barry:

Thank you for your letter and interest in Progress Energy and my role as CEO. I am happy to provide the enclosed responses to your questions.

I wish you the very best in reaching your goal of becoming a CEO one day.

Sincerely,

WCIII:dcj
Enclosure

Responses to Questions from Douglas Barry
From William Cavanaugh III, Chairman & CEO of Progress Energy
June 2003

1. Was there a turning point in your career that brought you down the path to become the leader you are today? If so, what was that point? Did you recognize it at the time?

> One early important "turning point" was my leadership training and experience in the U.S. Navy Nuclear Power Program under Admiral Rickover – just after I graduated from college. At the time I knew it was a significant experience, but I had no idea it would eventually lead to my being CEO of a large company.

2. What do I need to know beyond books and academics to become a leader?

- Deal with reality. In other words, learn to be clear and honest with yourself and others about the situation and challenges you (or your organization) faces.

- Commit to continual learning and improvement in everything you do. Never be complacent that you've completely mastered a skill or area of expertise. Be a life-long learner. Leaders continually "set the bar" higher when it comes to their own performance and that of the people they lead.

- Embrace diversity. Be open to the differences in people – not just differences of gender, race and ethnic origin, but diversity of ideas and ways of approaching problems and issues. Companies' workforces and customer bases are increasingly diverse. Successful leaders must learn to acknowledge, appreciate and harness those differences – view them as a source of strength, not weakness. (Douglas, your extensive travel undoubtedly has helped you learn about and appreciate the diversity of people and backgrounds.)

- Be disciplined in follow-through. Too often leaders set lofty goals but never focus on what's necessary to achieve the goals. It's important both to plan the work and to work the plan.

- Focus on people. Clearly, leaders must have strategic insight and understand how to achieve financial objectives and customer satisfaction. Equally important, leaders must be good at the "people side" – be able to select the right employees and then develop and motivate them to perform at their best.

GTE Corporation

January 26, 2000

1255 Corporate Drive
P.O.Box 152257
Irving, TX 75015-2257

Douglas Barry

Voorhees, NJ 08043

Dear Douglas:

How nice it was to hear from a 13-year-old who is interested in becoming a fellow CEO. As to your question, I believe CEOs need four basic traits to be successful in leading their companies:

First, they must lead with speed. Our world is changing more quickly every day. That creates tremendous opportunity, but CEOs must seize the moment.

Second, CEOs must dare to fail. A CEO who plays it safe all the time isn't setting goals that are high enough. Sometimes even the best-laid plans don't work. To me, though, failing to try something great is far worse than attempting something that fails.

Third, you must never be satisfied with just being the best. No matter how good a person gets at something, it's always possible to do even better.

Finally, the best CEOs build the team to achieve the dream. Even Michael Jordan needed teammates to play the game. He couldn't take on the New Jersey Nets alone. It's possible to fail by yourself, but success requires teamwork.

While these principles have served me well, there is another element to success that doesn't concern careers or material possessions. It's about being happy with who you are and what you have, even as you work hard to become better.

I also think success is about giving back, whether it's reciprocating emotions with loved ones or giving back to the community through volunteer service. As they say, you get what you give. That's true success.

Thanks for your letter. I look forward to seeing your name in the opening pages of a corporate annual report one day!

Best wishes,

Chuck Lee

CRL:rlp

Enc.

"Respect the dignity of everyone you meet irrespective of their race, beliefs, gender or social status. Each individual is sacred. The differences among us enrich our world. They are to be valued."

—BERTRAM SCOTT, PRESIDENT AND CEO, TIAA-CREF LIFE INSURANCE, NEW YORK, NY

"What is your relationship with God? Moral understanding is a lifelong process. One must have an anchor."

—JOHN TYSON, Chairman and CEO, Tyson Foods Inc., Springdale, AR

"I believe in people and think they are more effective when given principles rather than procedures, strategies rather than tactics, whys rather than wants."

—HARVEY GOLUB, CHAIRMAN AND CEO, AMERICAN EXPRESS CO., NEW YORK, NY

Give Something Back

"Actions need to go beyond the letter of the law to a spirit of trust and integrity, and a willingness to lead on issues where the needs are greatest. This also includes a commitment to give back to make the world a better place—both as a corporation and by providing opportunities for employees to give their time and talents to help others."

—BETSY HOLDEN, PRESIDENT AND CEO,
KRAFT FOODS NORTH AMERICA, NORTHFIELD, IL

"WORK HARD AT BEING FRIENDLY AND MAKING FRIENDS. HELP OTHERS WHO ARE LESS FORTUNATE. START NOW TO GET PERSONALLY INVOLVED IN COMMUNITY PROJECTS AND LEARN HOW YOU CAN MAKE A DIFFERENCE IN ANOTHER PERSON'S LIFE. THIS WILL REQUIRE SOME SACRIFICES, BUT THE REWARDS WILL BE GREAT."

—ROY W. HALEY, CEO, Wesco International, Pittsburgh, PA

"Learn every day . . . demand the most from yourself and others . . . [and] give back to your company and community."

—JEFFREY IMMELT, Chairman, General Electric Company, Fairfield, CT

"BE A SERVANT LEADER. I BELIEVE THAT AS A LEADER, ONE MUST HAVE A TRUE DESIRE TO SERVE IN ORDER TO BE EFFECTIVE. I SEE MY ROLE AS A SERVANT LEADER AS ONE THAT ENCOURAGES EMPLOYEES TO ALWAYS STRETCH THEIR ABILITIES TO THE NEXT LEVEL SO THAT THEY WILL GROW IN THEIR POSITIONS."

—JAMES F. PARKER, Vice Chairman and CEO, Southwest Airlines Co., Dallas, TX

SOUTHWEST AIRLINES CO.

James F. Parker
Vice Chairman and Chief Executive Officer

P.O. Box 36611
Dallas, Texas 75235-1611

June 18, 2003

Mr. Douglas Barry

Voorhees, NJ 08043

Dear Douglas:

Congratulations on pursuing your dream and for presenting such a passionate and articulate request for CEO responses. I also admire the tenacity it took for you to pursue this project even when your teachers were less than enthusiastic. Kudos to your parents for encouraging you.

From reading your letter, it sounds like you are taking some very deliberate steps to prepare now for the position to which you aspire. Also, I admire the fact that you are seeking "real world" advice from leaders across the spectrum of corporate America.

The turning point in my career was the first time I met Herb Kelleher, who, as you know, is the chairman of Southwest Airlines. We both practiced law in our former lives and met in 1977 while working on a case, each representing different parties in a fraud case. We discovered that we had a great deal in common, and I joined Herb's San Antonio law firm in 1979. It seemed natural after representing Southwest as outside counsel for years, that I join the Southwest corporate team in 1986. The rest, as they say, is history. Having a mentor like Herb--who is both brilliant in his business dealings and a true "leader" of people--has been a powerful and defining force in my life. However, I never aspired to be the CEO of Southwest Airlines, but rather was proud and passionate about the company and the opportunities I was given here. I was both surprised and honored when asked to take on the role.

As for leadership techniques that you won't find in textbooks: Be a servant leader. I believe that as a leader, one must have a true desire to serve in order to be effective. I see my role as a servant leader as one that encourages Employees to always stretch their abilities to the next level so that they will grow in their positions. Leaders at Southwest find themselves removing barriers to an individual's success instead of finding reasons to say no. We consistently encourage Employees to express their ideas on working smarter and more productively, and then they implement those ideas that work. All of this equates to Employees who find positions that allow them to do a job they are passionate about, and, therefore, they work harder at what they do--which equates in the longrun to extreme loyalty and high productivity, as well as an unmatched sense of ownership.

I wish you the best of luck in your compilation of the many responses you are sure to get. The list of CEOs you have already heard from is really impressive, and you seem to be a young man whose determination and creativity will ensure your book reaches the shelves! I look forward to reading it.

Sincerely,

James F. Parker

KRAFT FOODS INC.

Betsy D. Holden
Co-Chief Executive Officer, and
President and Chief Executive Officer
Kraft Foods North America

August 22, 2003

Mr. Douglas Barry

Voorhees, NJ 08043

Dear Douglas:

I received your letter earlier this summer and would be pleased to share some of my thoughts with you on career and leadership.

With all of the news over the past couple of years about corporate missteps and financial wrongdoing, it's nice to hear that young people like yourself still view the business world as a desirable career choice.

I spent most of my childhood in Pennsylvania, in a small town about 30 miles southwest of Pittsburgh. Like you, my father was a doctor and my mother worked in business as an accountant before she had children. My parents have been such an inspiration to me in all aspects of my life. One thing that they instilled in me from an early age is that you don't have to be the best but you have to try your best in everything. That has stayed with me in my career and in my personal life.

To your question about a turning point in my career…My turning point came fairly early in my career. My background is in education. I have both a bachelor's and master's degree in education and began my career as an elementary school teacher. I was also doing work with a toy manufacturer, developing educational teaching aids for toys. This brought me into contact with the marketing groups at the toy company and I thought that business and marketing looked like a lot of fun. So, I went back to school to get my MBA. At that point I knew I wanted to lead a business someday as CEO. It was my decision to change from teaching to business that brought me to Kraft more than 20 years ago and put me on the path to where I am today. Even today though, I continue to use my education background, especially as it pertains to working with groups and developing people within Kraft.

The topic of leadership is such an interesting one – and critical to the success of any business. Warren Bennis is one of my favorite authors/experts on the subject. In my career, I've given a lot of thought to the subject too, and believe that developing leadership talent is one of the key challenges facing business today. As I've talked to employees within Kraft and to many outside groups, I've encouraged them to take a 3-D view of leadership. Successful leaders need to develop their abilities to be outstanding business leaders, which includes setting the vision and mission, identifying the values and developing the strategies, goals and game plan. But that's just the starting point; only the first dimension of leadership.

There are two other dimensions to leadership that are just as important, if not more important, to success today -- people leadership and societal leadership. People leadership is the ability to hire and keep the best people, develop their skills, build teams and inspire and motivate excellence. It requires making a commitment to building a strong relationship between the company and the individual and it can create an incredible bond.

Societal leadership encompasses the company's relationship with the world around it. The leader tends to and guides that relationship, understanding public expectations and the role of the company in the world. Actions need to go beyond the letter of the law to a spirit of trust and integrity, and a willingness to lead on issues where the needs are greatest. This also includes a commitment to give back to make the world a better place – both as a corporation and by providing opportunities for employees to give their time and talents to help others.

I would encourage you to find opportunities to develop all three dimensions of leadership throughout your education, your work career and your life. If you think about it, you really are a CEO already– you're the CEO of Your Life. It's up to you to decide where you want to head in the future and then make it happen. I wish you the best of luck.

Sincerely,

Betsy Holden
Co-CEO, Kraft Foods Inc., and
President and CEO, Kraft Foods North America

Robert A. Eckert
CHAIRMAN &
CHIEF EXECUTIVE OFFICER

Mattel, Inc.

June 12, 2003

333 Continental Boulevard
Mail Stop: M1-1524
El Segundo, California 90245-5012

Mr. Douglas Barry

Voorhees, NJ 08043

Dear Douglas:

Greetings from Southern California, where I am sure you would enjoy the surfing.

I am writing in response to your recent letter requesting advice on leadership. As an aside, your letter was well written. You are quickly mastering English and your passion for writing is evident.

Like you, I am interested in leadership, and have studied the topic for many years. The following are three observations which you may find helpful to your understanding of leadership.

1. Leadership begins early in life. In my judgment, a small portion of leadership is innate. A much larger portion is environmental, with parents playing a huge role in developing the next generation of leaders. (Both you and I are products of a leadership-friendly family environment.) Finally, and most importantly, beyond the gene pool and the environment, successful leaders study, work diligently on and practice leadership.

2. Overcoming the natural Fear of Failure is important. In response to your first question regarding a "turning point," I did, indeed, have such an experience. Midway through my career, I was the leader of a business unit that was experiencing difficult times. At one point, rumors began circulating over "who's gonna get fired?" The most likely answer was me. Once I accepted that outcome, my energy focused exclusively on "how can I make this business succeed on my way out the door?" In other words, by accepting my fate, I no longer feared failure. Of course, the story had a good ending: the business turned around, and I was promoted, not fired.

3. "A leader is a dealer in hope." Napoleon said that. Hope is the most human of emotions. Only we know that the future can be different from the past. Successful leaders engender hope in their followers and appeal to their desire to create a better future.

Thanks for giving me the opportunity to support your examination of leadership. I am hopeful that it remains one of your favorite subjects.

Warmest regards,

Bob Eckert

Bob Eckert

"HOPE IS THE MOST HUMAN EMOTION. ONLY WE KNOW THE FUTURE CAN BE DIFFERENT FROM THE PAST. SUCCESSFUL LEADERS ENGENDER HOPE IN THEIR FOLLOWERS AND APPEAL TO THEIR DESIRE TO CREATE A BETTER FUTURE."

—BOB ECKERT, Chairman and CEO, Mattel Inc., El Segundo, CA

"FOCUS ON MAKING A CONTRIBUTION [INSTEAD OF] MAKING A CAREER."

—GERARD J. KLEISTERLEE, President and CEO, Royal Phillips Electronics, The Netherlands

"YOU WILL FIND AS A LEADER YOU HAVE TO GET THINGS DONE THROUGH PEOPLE AND WITH PEOPLE. WITHOUT THE SKILLS AND CAPABILITIES OF MOTIVATING THEM TO PURSUE YOUR IDEAS, YOU WILL FIND THE ROAD TO LEADERSHIP HAS A LOT OF ROADBLOCKS."

—ALBERT R. GAMPER JR., Chairman, President and CEO, CIT Group Inc., Livingston, NJ

"You make a living by what you get; you make a life by what you give. A leader knows this."

—PAT CROCE, former President, Philadelphia 76ers, Philadelphia, PA

A.G. Lafley
Chairman of the Board,
President and Chief Executive
The Procter & Gamble Company
1 Procter & Gamble Plaza
Cincinnati, Ohio 45202-3315
www.pg.com

May 22, 2003

Mr. Douglas Barry

Voorhees, NJ 08043

Dear Douglas:

Thanks for your letter of May 2. I want to say, first, how much I admire your initiative and your obvious desire to learn. I'm confident, given your achievements so far, that you will become an effective and inspiring leader.

You asked two questions:

1. Was there a turning point in your career that helped you down the path to become the leader you are today?

2. What do I need to know beyond books and academics to become a leader?

A pivotal experience for me was my service in the U.S. Navy, for two reasons.

First, I was given an opportunity to run the Post Exchange -- the on-post grocery and sundries store. This was my first business experience, and I loved the challenge. I was accountable for understanding and meeting the needs of customers -- sailors, spouses and families -- who relied on my store. I was responsible for running the operation profitably. And I was responsible for a small staff of colleagues who kept the store running day to day. That experience convinced me to pursue a career in business.

I also experienced the power of diversity in a way that I had not before. I was working with people from different backgrounds, with different personalities and styles, from different cultures. The Navy was a highly disciplined culture, of course, but discipline did not equal conformity -- and the best leaders I observed took advantage of diversity to get extraordinary results. Seeing and experiencing that approach helped shape my own leadership philosophy, and influences the way I lead yet today.

This brings me to your second question. Books and academics have an important role to play in your development as a leader, but there is no substitute for good coaching, good role models and personal experience. My advice is simple: Seek out and learn from all three. Find a college which values and nurtures personal leadership. For example, I chose Harvard Business School for my graduate work precisely because they said their entire curriculum was focused on developing the world's best operating general managers. Find work experiences where the people you'll work with have a passion for developing leaders, and seek out mentors who will provide candid, day-to-day coaching and feedback. And, finally, embrace a mindset of "humble

P&G

confidence" -- a belief in your abilities tempered by recognition that you must never stop learning to be and stay effective as a leader.

I'll close with a final observation. I believe great leaders are distinguished by four characteristics, and encourage you to consider these as you develop your own leadership skills:

- ❖ They have deeply held values that guide their choices. They articulate these values clearly and share them often.
- ❖ They deal with reality. They see things as they are, not as they would wish them to be.
- ❖ They embrace change. They see change as opportunity, not threat, and find creative ways to turn it to their advantage.
- ❖ They develop other leaders, and consider the real test of their leadership to be what happens when they're no longer around.

I hope these thoughts are helpful to you, Douglas. I wish you great success in your life and career.

All the best,

A. G. Lafley

AGL:kbk (0822)

What I've Learned

When I was in the eighth grade, I took on a very involved group history project.

At the outset, I assembled a team of my closest friends, and very soon began barking out orders and directions as if I knew what I was doing and thinking that everything would work out just fine. But I soon learned that, within a project or organization, people come into conflict with each other—there are disputes, problems, and all sorts of unseen factors that can cause things to go wrong. In order for us to produce a good project, I had to learn to act as a mediator of ideas and desires, to know when enough was enough, and to know when we should take breaks and play video games instead of pressing on.

My experience with group projects turned out to be a small-scale version of what takes place in a real corporation. From Mr. George Fisher's letter, in particular, I learned that the work environment must be amiable and enjoyable, one "in which everyone can contribute." People can be pushed to their limits, and this often produces a good product—however, if you push people too far, then you damage both the people and the environment in which they work. No one likes to be bossed around, and a good leader must know the difference between being a tyrant and being a strong leader who listens to his employees' problems and sees them through to good times.

One of the most surprising themes in these letters is that leaders work for their employees, and not the other way around. Mr. Parker said to "Be a servant leader." I realized that being at the top means that you have to work for those below to ensure that people remain happy, inspired, and productive. Being the boss is one thing, but being a compassionate individual who understands that people are not machines and cannot be pushed and shoved too far is really what being a good leader is all about.

Curiosity

LOOK, LISTEN, LEARN

cu.ri.os.i.ty **(noun):**
a desire to know and learn
—American Heritage Dictionary, 3rd Edition

"To be successful one must be willing to learn and apply new concepts and not be afraid of change."

—CRAIG R. BARRETT, CEO,
INTEL CORP., CHANDLER, AZ

School, you might say, is preparation for the real lessons in life. This, at least, is the conclusion I drew from the answers to this question asked of every executive I contacted: "What do I need beyond books and academics to become a good leader?" The common thread that linked all their answers can be summed up in one word: curiosity.

Curiosity, and satisfying it, is a course that takes a lifetime to complete. Nobody fails unless they drop out. And what's most inspiring is the fact that most of the CEOs stressed the importance of learning for its own sake as opposed to learning to make great grades and to win academic honors. Obviously, there is nothing wrong with going to the head of the class. But an even more important message is that even those in the back of the class—if they would apply their natural curiosity through a commitment to reading and learning—can reach the greatest heights.

On Curiosity:

The first and simplest emotion which we discover in
the human mind, is Curiosity. By curiosity, I mean
whatever desire we have for, or whatever pleasure
we take in, novelty. We see children perpetually running from place to place, to hunt out something new:
they catch with great eagerness, and with very little
choice, at whatever comes before them; their attention is engaged by everything, because everything
has, in that stage of life, the charm of novelty to recommend it. But as those things, which engage us
merely by their novelty, cannot attach for us any
length of time, curiosity is the most superficial of all
the affections; it changes its object perpetually, it has
an appetite which is very sharp, but very easily satisfied; and it has always an appearance of giddiness,
restlessness, and anxiety. Curiosity, from its nature,
is a very active principle; it quickly runs over the
greatest part of its objects, and soon exhausts the
variety which is commonly to be met with in nature;
the same things make frequent returns, and they
return with less and less of any agreeable effect. In
short, the occurrences of life, by the time we come
to know it a little, would be incapable of affecting the
mind with any other sensations than those of

loathing and weariness, if many things were not adapted to affect the mind by means of other powers besides novelty in them, and of other passions besides curiosity in ourselves. These powers and passions shall be considered in their place. But whatever these powers are, or upon what principle soever they affect the mind, it is absolutely necessary that they should not be exerted in those things which a daily and vulgar use have brought into a stale unaffecting familiarity. Some degree of novelty must be one of the materials in every instrument which works upon the mind; and curiosity blends itself more or less with all our passions.

—EDMUND BURKE, FROM *ON THE SUBLIME AND BEAUTIFUL*

ARAMARK CORPORATION

JOSEPH NEUBAUER
CHAIRMAN AND CHIEF EXECUTIVE OFFICER

February 7, 2000

Mr. Douglas Barry

Voorhees, NJ 08043

Dear Douglas:

Thank you for your letter regarding your class project. Attached is a recent
New York Times article on my background. In terms of the qualities which
helped prepare me to be a CEO, I would cite the following:

- Parents who made sure that I would have the best opportunities to
  achieve my dreams.

- Education from grade school through college which allowed me to
  think about the world in a broader context.

Thanks for your interest. Good luck on your project and in your other
schoolwork.

Sincerely,

JN/klp

Attachment

ARAMARK TOWER
1101 MARKET STREET
PHILADELPHIA, PA 19107-2988

The Power of Persistence

"Persistence best prepares someone for becoming a CEO. In the words of Calvin Coolidge, 'Nothing in the world can take the place of persistence. Talent will not; nothing is more common than unsuccessful men with talent. Genius will not; unrewarded genius is almost a proverb. Education will not; the world is full of educated derelicts. Persistence and determination alone are omnipotent.'"

—RICHARD L. SHARP, CHAIRMAN AND CEO,
CIRCUIT CITY STORES INC., RICHMOND, VA

"The more you know, the better equipped you will be to tackle all the obstacles you meet on your way to reaching your objectives."

—IVAN SEIDENBERG, Chairman and CEO,
Bell Atlantic Corp., New York, NY

"UNDERSTANDING THE HUMAN CONDITION IS ESSENTIAL TO BEHAVING IN A WAY THAT COMPELS OTHERS TO FOLLOW. A MOTIVATED INDIVIDUAL OF GOOD VALUES, WHO SEEKS GOALS IN THE WAY THAT INCORPORATE A THOROUGH UNDERSTANDING OF HUMAN NATURE, IS BOUND TO BE A GOOD LEADER."

—GARY LEACH, President, MRM Steel, Winnipeg, Canada

"KEEP YOURSELF BALANCED IN WORK, PLAY, STUDIES, RELIGIOUS AFFILIATIONS, AND HEALTH."

—HARRY M. JANSEN, CEO, Baxter International, Deerfield, IL

Bell Atlantic Corporation
1095 Avenue of the Americas
New York, NY 10036

Ivan Seidenberg
Chairman & Chief Executive Officer

January 25, 2000

Mr. Douglas Barry

Voorhees, NJ 08043

Dear Douglas:

I am responding to your letter requesting information on what it takes to become a successful CEO.

In order to become a success in your professional and personal lives, make education and continuous learning one of your primary goals. The more you know, the better equipped you will be to tackle all the obstacles you meet on your way to reaching your objectives. Also, embrace change. Although change in your life may seem scary at first, experiencing change will make you more resilient and adaptable to future events in your life. Continue to challenge yourself as you did with the sport of surfing. Any challenge you meet helps you to build confidence and character. Last, continue to hone your writing skills. I am very impressed with the letter you wrote to me.

Job experience is a requirement for becoming CEO, and this experience must be in a number of areas. Knowledge in Finance, Human Resources, Government Relations, Public Relations, and International Business would be helpful in obtaining your goal of becoming a CEO.

As for the present time, listen to your parents, pay attention in school, do your homework, admit when you are wrong, always do what you know is the right thing to do, and you are certain to be a success.

Sincerely yours,

Ivan Seidenberg

"LEARN YOUR CRAFT ONE STEP AT A TIME. DEDICATE YOURSELF TO THE DETAILS OF YOUR ENTERPRISE AND THE REST WILL TAKE CARE OF ITSELF."

—DR. JEAN-PIERRE GARNIER, CEO, GlaxoSmithKline, Durham, NC

"... I am still learning. That is an important mark of a good leader ... to know you don't know it all and never will."

—ANNE M. MULCAHY, CEO, Xerox, Stamford, CT

"[NOWADAYS] YOU'LL NEED AN INTERNATIONAL EDUCATION AND AT LEAST A FEW YEARS ABROAD. THIS WILL HELP YOU TO UNDERSTAND DIFFERENT CULTURES AND HOW THE GLOBALIZED BUSINESS WORKS TODAY—ESPECIALLY BETWEEN HUMAN BEINGS FROM DIFFERENT CULTURES."

—KLAUS ZUMWINKEL, CEO, Deutsche Post World Net, Bonn, Germany

"Must" Win Situation

Q: What do I need to know beyond books and academics to become a leader?

A:
- You must have deductive logic to solve problems
- You must have an explicit strategy [that is] well communicated
- You must always get the facts and be persistent
- You must build a strong team

—DON WASHKEWICZ, PRESIDENT AND CEO,
PARKER HANNIFIN CORPORATION, CLEVELAND, OH

Lawrence K. Fish
Chairman
President and Chief Executive Officer

One Citizens Plaza
Providence, RI 02903

Citizens Bank Building
28 State Street
Boston, MA 02109

May 27, 2003

Mr. Douglas Barry

Voorhees, NJ 08043

Dear Doug

Let me begin by telling you how much I admire your mother and how you can learn a great deal from her leadership skills and energy. She has devoted herself enthusiastically to Citizens, and I am a grateful colleague.

I also admire the maturity of your letter. I have a daughter who is only a year or two younger than you, and I hope she, next year (her Junior year), writes with the same skill that you exhibit in your letter.

I believe in emotional intelligence. I think the skills that a leader most need are empathy, persistence and decisiveness. I have known many people who were smarter than me, but very few who could outwork me. I never give up. I care deeply about people. And, most of all, I love grabbing the reigns, being the boss, making the calls.

I think the turning point was following graduation from Drake University. I was selected for the Class of 1968 at Harvard Business School. I knew Harvard was good. I struggled to get through. Though I didn't recognize it at the time, those struggles raised my sights. Harvard made me think big thoughts, showed me how special I could be. I never looked back and drove ferociously and uninterruptedly toward the top.

I have learned little from books. It seems to me that the more you lead, the easier it gets. Today, I find that I am like a car going down a hill -- the more I take my foot off the accelerator, the faster the car goes. Getting to this point had nothing to do with teachers or books. Find life experiences and swallow them whole. Travel. Meet many people. Go down some dead ends and explore some dark alleys. Try everything. Exhaust yourself in the glorious pursuit of life.

My favorite quote is by Teddy Roosevelt:

"It is not the critic who counts, not the man who points out how the strong man stumbled, or where the doer of deeds could have done them better. The credit belongs to the man who is actually in the arena: whose face is marred by dust and sweat and blood; who strives valiantly; who errs and comes short again and again; who knows the great enthusiasms, the great devotions, and spends himself in a worthy cause; who, at the best, knows in the end the triumph of high achievement; and who, at the worst, if he fails, at least fails while daring greatly, so that his place shall never be with those cold and timid souls who know neither victory nor defeat. "

Based on your letter, the journey to the top for you has already begun.

Best of luck.

Sincerely,

LKF/mc

Corbin A. McNeill, Jr.
Chairman, President and
Chief Executive Officer

PECO Energy Company
2301 Market Street
PO Box 8699
Philadelphia, PA 19101-8699

February 24, 2000

Mr. Douglas Barry

Vorhees, NJ 08043

Dear Douglas:

I am never too busy to answer questions from students, and I am delighted to assist you in your class project concerning the attributes of leadership.

I believe many of the qualities that best prepared me for business leadership were the qualities I learned as a student, particularly at the United States Naval Academy. They included identifying the right people for the task at hand, giving them not only the responsibility but also the authority and the resources to complete the task, letting them know clearly they are responsible for results, and supporting and encouraging them throughout their work.

Effective leadership also demands personal qualities like integrity, boldness, creativity, accountability and the strong commitment to continuous learning. Leadership requires, at times, the willingness to explore ideas and concepts beyond the traditional ways we have always managed; the willingness to take chances, to fail, and to go right back and try again.

You described yourself as an ambitious young man, and that's good, because ambition, in the context of a personal drive to study, learn, work hard and achieve, is also a very important component of developing into an effective business leader. Also, attempting to follow in the footsteps of your mother, and being guided by her advise and counsel, sounds to me like a very good idea.

Thanks, Douglas, for asking me to assist you, and good luck in all your future endeavors.

Sincerely,

Carl McNeill

"LEADERSHIP HAS LESS TO DO WITH WALKING IN FRONT AND LEADING THE WAY THAN IT DOES WITH LISTENING TO THE NEEDS OF THE PEOPLE OF THE COMPANY AND MEETING THEM."

—CHARLES M. CAWLEY, Chairman and CEO, MBNA America, Wilmington, DE

"THE TRUE LEADER IS ALWAYS LISTENING, LEARNING AND BEING TRULY OPEN TO THE WORLD AROUND HIM."

—JAY GELLERT, CEO, Healthnet, Inc., Woodland Hills, CA

"I believe that getting the most you can out of your life experiences is probably the best way to prepare to be a leader."

—HENRY A. MCKINNELL, CHAIRMAN AND CEO, PFIZER INC., NEW YORK, NY

Beyond Books . . .

Q: What do I need to know beyond books and academics to become a leader?

A:
- Trust in people and have confidence in their judgment and integrity.
- Willingness to work hard, challenge ideas and persevere until the goal is met.
- Intellectual curiosity and a commitment to continuous learning.

—EDWARD LIDDY, CEO,
ALLSTATE, NORTHBROOK, IL

"True leaders are always listening and learning."

—JAY M. GELLERT, President and CEO, Health Net Inc., Woodland Hills, CA

"GETTING TO THIS POINT HAD NOTHING TO DO WITH TEACHERS OR BOOKS. FIND LIFE EXPERIENCES AND SWALLOW THEM WHOLE. TRAVEL. MEET MANY PEOPLE. GO DOWN SOME DEAD ENDS AND EXPLORE SOME DARK ALLEYS. TRY EVERYTHING. EXHAUST YOURSELF IN THE GLORIOUS PURSUIT OF LIFE."

—LAWRENCE K. FISH, Chairman, President and CEO, Citizens Financial Group, Inc., Boston, MA

"I am curious and interested in just about everything. So, I am always learning and working at the margin of my ignorance."

—HARVEY GOLUB, CEO, American Express, New York, NY

GirlScouts
of Southeastern Pennsylvania

Douglas Barry

Voorhees, NJ 08043

August 28, 2003

Dear Doug:

I apologize for the length of time I have taken to respond to your request for information on my experiences in becoming a leader. I only wish that the thoughts below were of such a profound nature that you'd say "no wonder it took so long". Unfortunately, they aren't, but they are sincere and, therefore, I hope, useful.

"Turning point…."

I think there was no single turning point for me in becoming a leader but a gradual recognition that I could have an influence on the direction of an organization or a project if I stepped forward and took responsibility. Often in these situations there was an absence of someone clearly taking the lead (even if there was a designated "leader") or willingness to say "I will" from others. In these instances, colleagues welcomed my stepping forward. I think that I have learned that people are hungry for leadership, especially when they feel committed to getting something done or are concerned about the welfare of the project or organization.

Leadership can be demonstrated in many ways. As I have grown more confident as a leader, I have learned how to adapt to diverse situations and to use different tools and styles. Sometimes leading requires giving direction but, more often, it involves guiding or creating a structure or process to enable those you are "leading" to be successful in making something happen, achieving a goal, or solving a problem. I have also learned that the most gifted leaders create the symbols that inspire others and which can communicate the ideals that are worth working together to realize. It takes experience and confidence to know which style serves most effectively and lots of practice to be able to use them well.

Mailing address:
PO Box 27540
Philadelphia, PA 19118

www.gssp.org

 Girl Scouts. A United Way Agency

"Tools"

Observing leaders at work is the most powerful teaching tool there is. Look for leaders in all kinds of situations and think about how they do what they do and how you and others respond. The theory and case studies in books and courses is supplemental and helps to create a context of theory but practice is best. So watch and learn and, to quote Nike, "Just do it".

I have every confidence that you will be an effective and thoughtful leader wherever you are, so I wish you good luck as you pursue this project and all else you undertake.

Sincerely,

Sharon A. Smith
CEO

Street-Smart Advice

From the chairman and CEO of Crown, Cork & Seal Co. Inc., Philadelphia, PA:

Dear Doug,

It is obvious from your letter that you are very intelligent. Use this gift with the addition of common sense often referred to as "street smarts." Combine the two and your desires in life will be accomplished.

Sincerely,
William J. Avery

What I've Learned

I have always been a good student, and I have applied myself (as most students do) in order to enjoy good grades when my report card comes around.

And while a lot of the advice I got from these letters stressed the importance of scholastics, it did so in a surprising way. It is more important, it seems, to learn more out of a genuine curiosity and craving for knowledge than merely for the sake of getting a 4.0 stamped onto your record.

I have heard that no one ever has to stop learning; people are capable of learning and bettering themselves at any age. Mr. Golub expressed this idea in saying that he is "curious and interested in just about everything" and, as a result of this curiosity, he is "always learning and working at the margin of his ignorance." That statement taught me a valuable lesson: that even a man who has accomplished so much, who has learned so much and has become so successful, still views himself as ignorant in some ways and capable of learning new things.

I've known many people who are too proud of their accomplishments and feel that, once they've accomplished a certain goal, the learning and the growing is over. But one single goal is never enough, and in order to keep pushing the limits and reaching for new heights, you have to acquire more and more knowledge. Ideas and inspiration can be found almost anywhere and, following the logic of Mr. Gellert, a good leader is "always listening, learning, and being truly open to the world around him." Close-mindedness is never conducive to the learning experience. The greatest of all thinkers and philosophers have borrowed ideas from one another and expanded on them. A good leader learns from the mistakes he or she makes, and from the mistakes made by his or her peers, and works hard to better a situation based on those past failures or even past accomplishments. The point is, there's always something better, something more developed, and as a result of our inability as human beings to attain perfection, we must simply be content with being constantly open minded and curious.

It's also important to realize, as a student or even as someone who's out of school, that all the lessons you learn in life will not necessarily be learned in a classroom. Mr. McKinnell expressed the fact that life experiences serve as "the best way to prepare to be a leader." Learning takes place everywhere and at every moment, and ignoring the lessons that take place outside of a classroom will cause you to miss out on some of the most important lessons of life. The person who admits weakness and ignorance, and works to better that weakness, succeeds more often than the person who believes the learning process ceases after and outside of school or the workplace.

Integrity

HONESTY ABOVE ALL, TO ALL

in.teg.ri.ty **(noun)**:
steadfast adherence to a strict
moral or ethical code.

—American Heritage Dictionary, 3rd Edition

"You cannot have a little integrity or a lot of integrity. There is no sliding scale for integrity. You either have it, or you don't."

—ROSEMARIE GRECO, DIRECTOR, OFFICE OF HEALTH CARE REFORM, HARRISBURG, PA

Honesty, these days, is not an attribute one can automatically assume to be part of a CEO's character and belief system. At least this is a conclusion that can be drawn from business headlines over the last few years. Whether recent corporate scandals involved leaders who distorted facts, rationalized questionable decisions, blamed subordinates for inappropriate behavior, or outright lied, the resulting loss of integrity has certainly proved unrecoverable. Integrity is something that needs to be earned every day, with every decision. Because at the end of the day, we are the choices we make.

The best leaders realize that their personal integrity level reflects upon the company as a whole. And ultimately, they understand that making integrity a top priority is as crucial as keeping a strong bottom line.

On Integrity:

The principle by which we naturally either approve
or disapprove of our own conduct, seems to be alto-
gether the same with that by which we exercise the
like judgments concerning the conduct of other people. We either approve or disapprove of the conduct
of another man according as we feel that, when we
bring his case home to ourselves, we either can or
cannot entirely sympathize with the sentiments and
motives which directed it. And, in the same manner,
we either approve or disapprove of our own conduct,
according as we feel that, when we place ourselves in
the situation of another man, and view it, as it were,
with his eyes and from his station, we either can or
cannot entirely enter into and sympathize with the
sentiments and motives which influenced it. We can
never survey our own sentiments and motives, we
can never form any judgment concerning them;
unless we remove ourselves, as it were, from our
own natural station, and endeavour to view them as
at a certain distance from us. . . . We endeavour to
examine our own conduct as we imagine any other
fair and impartial spectator would examine it. If,
upon placing ourselves in his situation, we thor-
oughly enter into all the passions and motives which

influenced it, we approve of it, by sympathy with the approbation of this supposed equitable judge. If otherwise, we enter into his disapprobation, and condemn it.

In the same manner our first moral criticisms are exercised upon the characters and conduct of other people; and we are all very forward to observe how each of these affects us. But we soon learn, that other people are equally frank with regard to our own. We become anxious to know how far we deserve their censure or applause, and whether to them we must necessarily appear those agreeable or disagreeable creatures which they represent us. We begin, upon this account, to examine our own passions and conduct, and to consider how these must appear to them, by considering how they would appear to us if in their situation. We suppose ourselves the spectators of our own behaviour, and endeavour to imagine what effect it would, in this light, produce upon us. This is the only looking-glass by which we can, in some measure, with the eyes of other people, scrutinize the propriety of our own conduct.

—ADAM SMITH, FROM *THE THEORY OF THE MORAL SENTIMENTS*

Three Keys to Leadership

Q: What do I need to know beyond books and academics to become a leader?

A:
- Integrity—first and foremost.
- Listening—the ability to focus and comprehend what's being communicated.
- Objectivity—the ability to receive information unbiased by previous experiences.

—RICHARD E. OLSON, CEO,
CHAMPION INTERNATIONAL, STAMFORD, CT

THE PEPSI BOTTLING GROUP

JOHN T. CAHILL
CHAIRMAN & CHIEF EXECUTIVE OFFICER

June 26, 2003

Mr. Douglas Barry

Voorhees, NJ 08043

Dear Douglas:

I enjoyed reading your letter of May 27, explaining your interest in business and particularly in the role CEOs play in leading their people and their organizations to success. I was pleased to hear you had such a great response from CEOs willing to share their views –and I will be glad to join them with my answers to your insightful questions.

The turning point in my career took place in 1985. I was 28 years old with four years of business experience under my belt, and big aspirations, similar to those you've outlined in your letter. At that time, I got my first taste of what it means to run a business—with responsibility not only for profit and loss, but for the people associated with the results. I was given a chance, relatively early in my career with RKO General, to take over as President of RKO Hotels, when a series of hotel partnerships were failing. My mission was to turn the situation around. Beyond case studies in graduate school, this was my first practical experience in understanding how to put all the pieces together in order to buck the trend and to get things moving in a positive direction. I learned a lot—and quickly—about what it takes to run a business. While education can give you a great foundation, it's the on the job experience that really brings it all home. At the time I knew that this was what I wanted to do, although I'm not sure until I looked back on the moment that I realized it was a turning point for me. The situation gave me perspective and helped me to build my confidence, two characteristics I would say are essential for strong leadership.

While a love of learning—in both formal and informal settings—is a hallmark of great leaders in every industry, what I believe guides you far beyond what's found in any book is your internal compass. Great values never go out of style. How you deal with adversity, how you cope with unexpected circumstances, and mostly, how you treat other people, are the most important aspects of leadership. These factors determine your leadership style, how people perceive you and, to a great extent, the type of legacy you will leave when your days as a CEO are over. In my opinion, what you know is very important, but what you do and how you do it are even more crucial to your ultimate success.

I have no doubt you will be successful, Douglas. Wanting it is half the battle.

I'm enclosing some coupons so you and your family can enjoy some of our great Pepsi beverages. Thank you for your interest in The Pepsi Bottling Group and in my point of view. I wish you much success with your schoolwork and your writing career. And, in the years to come, I'll be looking for your name among the leaders of the Fortune 500.

Regards,

John Cahill

THE PEPSI BOTTLING GROUP   1 PEPSI WAY, SOMERS, NY 10589

The Estēe Lauder Companies Inc.
767 Fifth Avenue
New York, NY 10153

Leonard A. Lauder
Chairman

February 3, 2000

Mr. Douglas Barry

Voorhees, NJ 08043

Dear Douglas,

Thank you so much for your very nice letter. Yes, I am a very busy person, but never too busy to respond to such a thoughtful, intelligent request. I agree with your "nothing ventured, nothing gained" attitude, and admire your ambition. There aren't too many people who realize at such an early age what their life's ambition is.

I have enclosed for you the principals of the Estée Lauder Companies. These are the same principles that my mother, Mrs. Estée Lauder, lived by, founded the company upon, and raised her two sons by. You see I followed in my mother's footsteps, just as you want to do.

Write me again when you are in college, as I'd like to see how you are doing, and if you still are headed in the same direction. Best of luck.

With kind regards.

Sincerely,

Leonard A. Lauder

LAL/bz

P.S.   Keep entering the surfing competition in Avalon. With your perseverance, I bet you'll win it some day!

Encl.

OUR PRINCIPLES

- Strive for Excellence – deliver your best.

- Put your customer first. Know your customers, understand their needs, and surpass their expectations.

- Be passionate about what you do! Enthusiasm and energy are contagious.

- Never stop caring. Show concern and respect for every individual, regardless of position or title.

- Understand your role in the big picture. We're all part of a larger whole.

- Look for new and better ways to do things to continually raise our standards.

- Communicate! Voice your ideas, share your concerns, pass on what you know, and be honest.

- Be a team player. We're stronger when we work together.

- Listen when others speak. Good ideas can come from anywhere.

- Be flexible. Success depends upon a willingness to adapt when situations change.

- Pay attention to the details – little things <u>do</u> make a difference.

- Solve the real problem, don't treat the symptom.

- Spread the good news. Let others know when they've done a good job.

- Smile…and have fun!

ESTÉE LAUDER COMPANIES

Ethics Breeds Trust

"It is critically important to be determined to do the right thing—to commit to conducting yourself with the highest standards of ethics and integrity. It will inspire people's confidence and trust in you. And people, as a result, will help you in ways that you would never expect, and maybe never even know about. They will go to great lengths to help you accomplish your goals. They will solve problems on your behalf. They will come to your defense when you are in trouble, which will happen from time to time. If you work for them, they will promote you."

—RAYMOND V. GILMARTIN,
CHAIRMAN, PRESIDENT AND CEO,
MERCK & CO., WHITEHOUSE STATION, NJ

"WHO YOU ARE, WHAT YOUR VALUES ARE, WHAT YOU STAND FOR. . . . THEY ARE YOUR ANCHOR, YOUR NORTH STAR. YOU WON'T FIND THEM IN A BOOK. YOU'LL FIND THEM IN YOUR SOUL."

—ANNE MULCAHY, CEO, Xerox Corporation, Stamford, CT

"Be selective about where you work, and make sure you're comfortable with what the company stands for, what it represents, and that it's something you can really commit yourself to."

—WILLIAM C. WELDON, CHAIRMAN AND CEO, JOHNSON AND JOHNSON, NEW BRUNSWICK, NJ

"GREAT VALUES NEVER GO OUT OF STYLE."

—JOHN T. CAHILL, Chairman and CEO, The Pepsi Bottling Group, Somers, NY

"GIVING HONEST VALUE FOR WHATEVER JOB YOU DO EARNS THE RESPECT OF THE PEOPLE YOU WORK FOR, THE PEOPLE YOU WORK WITH, AND LATER, THE PEOPLE WHO WORK FOR YOU."

—CARLOS M. GUTIERREZ, President and CEO, Kellogg Company, Battle Creek, MI

Federated
DEPARTMENT STORES, INC.

7 West Seventh Street · Cincinnati, Ohio 45202-2471

JAMES M. ZIMMERMAN
CHAIRMAN & CHIEF EXECUTIVE OFFICER

February 15, 2000

Mr. Douglas Barry

Voorhees, New Jersey 08043

Dear Douglas:

In response to your request for my thoughts on what leadership qualities best prepared me for becoming CEO of Federated Department Stores, Inc., I have to say first that I was most impressed with your letter. And your resume. For someone 13 years old, you have quite a few accomplishments that would be significant for someone twice your age. I'm just glad that by the time you're ready to take over the CEO's office, I'll be ready to retire...I wouldn't want to be competing with you!

As to your question, I would say that they most important qualities are the following:

- An ability to recognize and bring out the best talents and strengths of people working around you. No one gets to the top by himself or herself, and if that's your goal you'll get there sooner by listening to advice from those who know more about certain subjects that you do, from valuing their contributions and letting them know it.

- Perseverance. Nothing in the competitive world of business is easy, but accomplishment usually results from knowing what you want to achieve and not giving up when inevitable obstacles get in the way.

- Flexibility. Just as important as perseverance is the ability to adapt. Sometimes getting from point A to point B <u>will</u> require a few detours, and it's necessary to accommodate the unexpected. Change can be a positive, and as such it can be a catalyst for new growth and innovation, but it has to be managed. As CEO -- or to get to be CEO -- managing change within the organization is one of the most essential components of your job.

I hope this is helpful to you, for your class project and in your life. I have no doubt, Douglas, that you will be successful in whatever you choose to do.

Best of luck to you. Your parents must be special people – and very proud.

Sincerely,

Macy's • Bloomingdale's • The Bon Marché   Bloomingdale's by Mail, Ltd. • Macy's by Mail
Burdines • Goldsmith's • Lazarus • Rich's • Stern's   Macys.Com • Fingerhut

"Stand up for what's right, in small matters and large ones, and always do what you promise."

—REUBEN MARK, Chairman and CEO, Colgate-Palmolive Company, New York, NY

"AS CHIEF EXECUTIVE OFFICER OF A PUBLIC COMPANY, YOU ARE RESPONSI-BLE TO SHAREHOLDERS FOR THE CARE AND GROWTH OF THE ORGANIZATION'S ASSETS, AND JUST AS IMPORTANT, FOR THE PEOPLE WHO ARE YOUR FELLOW EMPLOYEES. I HAVE ALWAYS BELIEVED THAT PEOPLE ARE THE MOST IMPOR-TANT PART OF ANY ORGANIZATION, AND TO LEAD PEOPLE SUCCESSFULLY THEY NEED TO TRUST YOU AND YOUR COMMITMENT TO THEM AND TO THE ORGANIZATION AS A WHOLE."

—LAWRENCE A. WEINBACH, Chairman, President and CEO, Unisys, Blue Bell, PA

"Live each day as if your actions would be the headlines the next day in your local newspaper."

—JON A. BOSCIA, Chairman and CEO, Lincoln Financial Group, Philadelphia, PA

"LEARN TO DO WHAT OUGHT TO BE DONE, WHEN IT SHOULD BE DONE, WHETHER YOU LIKE IT OR NOT."

—ROY W. HALEY, CEO, Wesco International, Pittsburgh, PA

"Dedicate yourself to build a company, a product line, a competitive advantage . . . and with success will come opportunities to exercise more leadership."

—DR. JEAN-PIERRE GARNIER, CEO, GLAXOSMITHKLINE, DURHAM, NC

"Hard work, along with honesty, respect and confidence, make up a strong plan for success."

—CARLOS M. GUTIERREZ, President and CEO, Kellogg Company, Battle Creek, MI

Integral Objective

Q: What do I need to know beyond books and academics to become a leader?

A: Without a doubt, beyond books and academics, maintaining one's integrity should be the prime objective, and should remain so throughout life.

—J. TERRENCE LANNI, Chairman and CEO,
MGM Mirage, Las Vegas, NV

Sprint

William T. Esrey
Chairman
Chief Executive Officer

P.O. Box 11315
Kansas City, MO 64112

January 13, 2000

Mr. Douglas Berry

Voorhees, NJ 08043

Dear Douglas:

Thank you for your letter and inquiry for additional information.

Enclosed please find an article, which was recently written about me in the *Kansas City Star* that answers a lot of your questions. In addition, I would suggest that you become familiar with the Internet. By accessing the Internet you will be able to find a great deal of background information on a number of public persons.

I would just comment that if your ambition is to become a CEO, I would not concentrate on selecting a particular college or taking a particular course. Becoming a CEO is not a difficult task. In fact, you could form your own company and appoint yourself as CEO. Of greater importance is setting out in life what you want to achieve in terms of your personal objectives, then preparing yourself through education, experience and observations to achieve your aspirations.

Finally, attributes that will help you along the way no matter what profession you choose are integrity, hard work, independent thinking and observation, and conducting each and every day of your life with high ethical standards. Remember, an individual does not become a leader of an organization unless that person is respected and held in high regard by those that are going to be led.

Sincerely,

William T. Esrey

Encl.

"Integrity does not have a switch—you can't turn it on and off. A leader must always walk the talk . . . if he or she expects others to follow."

—PAT CROCE, former President, Philadelphia 76ers, Philadelphia, PA

"WE NEED THE COURAGE NOT ONLY TO STAND FOR SOMETHING, WE NEED THE COURAGE TO DO SOMETHING ABOUT WHAT WE STAND FOR, FOR THE COURAGE TO SPEAK OUT ON THE CRITICAL ISSUES THAT CONFRONT AND CONFOUND OUR ORGANIZATIONS AND OUR SOCIETY. WE CAN'T SHOW COURAGE IF WE KEEP OUR IDEAS AND OUR CONVICTIONS TO OURSELVES."

—JUDITH RODIN, President, University of Pennsylvania, Philadelphia, PA

"A successful leader models the way for his team. There is nothing more unifying than a set of values that are shared among all members of the team. A true leader brings the team together under the things it values most."

—JAMES H. BLANCHARD, CHAIRMAN AND CEO, SYNOVUS, COLUMBUS, OH

Honesty—Unconditionally

"There is nothing more important in a leader than a firm ethical grounding. A leader, particularly a public company CEO, must be committed to absolute integrity and honesty in the operation of his/her company. This, above all else, means telling the truth even when it may hurt. Honesty and integrity must be continually upheld and practiced through the rest of your academic career as well as your professional career."

—JACK O. BOVENDER JR., CHAIRMAN AND CEO, HCA, NASHVILLE, TN

"Be valued and principle based. Know what you stand for, and live by those standards."

—GEORGE M.C. FISHER, Chairman of the Board, Eastman Kodak Co., Rochester, NY

"HONESTY AND HARD WORK ARE STILL THE KEY TO SUCCESS. DO NOT STAY IN A WORK OR SOCIAL ENVIRONMENT WHERE YOU ARE NOT ENCOURAGED TO DO WHAT IS RIGHT."

—J. KENNETH GLASS, President and CEO, First Tennessee Bank, Memphis, TN

"No one wants to work with a chisler! Be honest with yourself and others as well."

—JEREMIAH J. SHEEHAN, CEO, Reynolds Metals, Richmond, VA

What I've Learned

Integrity was clearly the most important
and essential of all the traits mentioned
in these letters.

No matter what any of the CEO's wrote about, almost every one commented in some way about the need for honesty and integrity in one's career and life. It's very clear that lying is never an acceptable way to deal with an issue, and if you let yourself fall into the habit of being dishonest, then dishonesty becomes your mode of thinking. Mr. Croce told me that integrity wasn't like a switch—"you can't turn it on and off." Once you take the course of dishonesty, you cannot easily break away from that path. And if people find you to be an untrustworthy individual, they will not find it easy to trust you in the future, even when you are telling the complete truth.

Leaders who are honest and candid inspire people. It is hard to follow someone who has no integrity and no morals, because you will always be unsure of the person you are following. Leaders have to build a relationship with their employees based on trust, and there can be no surprises along the way. Everything must be honest and straightforward for success to be truly won. Many CEOs admit that the quick and simple way out is often seductive, but to a person, they understand that such a short-term solution is no solution at all.

Sometimes I want so badly to cheat on a test or copy a term paper because I simply do not want to do the work. There are so many other things I'd rather do, and if I only cheated this once then I would be in the clear for a while. The truth is, there are always going to be challenges; they just never stop coming at you. And when a challenge arises, you must ask yourself the crucial question of whether or not you are comfortable in lying to yourself and your colleagues. In my case, I've never gotten past the fact that if I cheated then the work would not be my own and my grade would be a fraud. Mr. Roy Haley put it quite simply, saying that sometimes you just have to do what you have to do "whether you like it or not."

Pragmatism

KNOW WHAT YOU DON'T KNOW

prag.ma.tism (noun):
a practical, matter-of-fact way of approaching
or assessing situations or of solving problems
—American Heritage Dictionary, 3rd Edition

"An important mark of a good leader [is] to know you don't know it all and never will."

—ANNE M. MULCAHY, CEO,
XEROX CORP., STAMFORD, CT

H umble is hardly a word I would have chosen to describe a person in such a lofty position as CEO. Was I ever wrong! I didn't actually come across that exact word too many times in the letters I received, but the spirit of humility came across loud and clear. All successful leaders may not be totally down-to-earth, but they certainly seem to hover close enough to it. Specifically, they do not consider themselves to be above others. In fact, it becomes apparent that conscientious, humble, pragmatic leaders spend their energy lifting others up rather than exalting themselves. And it becomes apparent that these are the leaders who are most capable of lifting up entire companies.

On Pragmatism:

You frequently desire me to give you some Advice, in Writing. There is, perhaps, no other valuable Thing in the World, of which so great a Quantity is given, and so little taken. Men do not generally err in their Conduct so much through Ignorance of their Duty, as thro In attention to their own Faults, or thro strong Passions and bad Habits; and, therefore, till that Inattention is cured, or those Passions reduced under the Government of Reason, Advice is rather resented as a Reproach, than gratefully acknowledged and followed.

Supposing then, that from the many good Sermons you have heard, good Books read, and good Admonitions received from your Parents and others, your Conscience is by this Time pretty well informed, and capable of advising you, if you attentively listen to it, I shall not fill this Letter with Lessons or Precepts of Morality and Religion; but rather recommend to you, that in order to obtain a clear Sight and constant Sense of your Errors, you would set apart a Portion of every Day for the Purpose of Self-Examination, and trying your daily Actions by that Rule of Rectitude implanted by GOD in your Breast. The properest Time for this, is when you are retiring to Rest; then carefully review the Transactions of the past Day; and consider how far they have agreed with what you know of your Duty to God and to Man, in the several Relations you stand in of a Subject to the Government, Servant to your Master, a Son, a Neighbour, a Friend, etc. When, by this Means, you have discovered the Faults of the Day, acknowledge them to God, and humbly beg of him not only Pardon for what is past, but Strength to fulfil your solemn Resolutions of guarding against them for the Future. Observing this Course steadily for some Time, you will find (through God's Grace assisting) that your Faults are continually diminishing, and your Stock of Virtue encreasing; in Consequence of which you will grow in Favour both with GOD and Man.

I repeat it, that for the Acquirement of solid, uniform, steady Virtue, nothing contributes more, than a daily strict SELF-EXAMINATION, by the Lights of Reason, Conscience, and the Word of GOD; joined with firm Resolutions of amending what you find amiss, and fervent Prayer for Grace and Strength to execute those Resolutions.

—BENJAMIN FRANKLIN, FROM *WRITINGS*

Sanford I. Weill
*Chairman & Co-Chief
Executive Officer*

Citigroup Inc.
153 East 53rd Street
New York, NY 10043

January 31, 2000

Mr. Douglas Barry

Voorhees, NJ 08043

Dear Douglas:

Letters like yours make me feel good, but also humble. It's nice to be asked about the keys to success, but I am afraid there are no secrets. I don't think that there is a magic key that works for everybody. I can share what I have always tried to do and hope that something might be helpful.

First, have I have tried to have a bias toward action. I try to do my homework, and then make decisions faster, rather than slower.

Second, I believe in treating other people with respect. My style is to speak to people, be available to them and willing to answer their questions. This also means being straightforward and honest with them.

Related to this is making partners. I try to make others feel part of what I am doing and to find ways of including them in the rewards of their contributions to success.

Finally, I believe that family is critical to success, so I have tried to keep my wife involved and informed in what I am thinking and doing. For me, she has been my most important partner.

Maybe some of these ideas will bring good luck in your future. From your letter, it seems that you have made a great start.

Sincerely,

Sandy Weill

"A CEO must dare to fail. A CEO who plays it safe all the time isn't setting goals that are high enough."

—CHARLES R. LEE, CHAIRMAN AND CEO, GTE CORP., IRVINGTON, TX

"Leaders are humble individuals. They don't seek the spotlight. They respect the others on the team."

—JOHN TYSON, Chairman and CEO, Tyson Foods Inc., Springdale, AR

"SUCCESSFUL LEADERS USUALLY KNOW WHAT THEY DON'T KNOW AND DEPEND ON OTHERS FOR SPECIFIC SOLUTIONS."

—CRAIG BARRETT, CEO, Intel Corp., Chandler, AZ

Four Star Qualities

Q: What qualities best prepared you for becoming a CEO?

A:
- Get a job while you are young
- Never know all the answers
- Trust your instincts
- Street smarts

—MILLARD S. DREXLER, CEO,
GAP, INC., SAN FRANCISCO, CA

EASTMAN

EARNEST W. DEAVENPORT, JR.
Chairman and Chief Executive Officer

Eastman Chemical Company
P.O. Box 511
Kingsport, Tennessee 37662-5075

February 15, 2000

MR DOUGLAS BARRY

VOORHEES NJ 08043

Dear Douglas:

Thank you for your letter concerning qualities that prepared me for becoming a CEO. I am delighted that you are interested in business leadership. And thanks for enclosing your resume. Looks like you are doing the right things to prepare yourself to follow in your mom's footsteps.

Here's my list:

1. First and foremost is a solid work ethic. My parents ran the local Western Auto store, so I was introduced early to the importance of work.

2. The second is the willingness to take reasonable risks. I was impressed that your resume demonstrates you are willing to take on challenges.

3. Finally, getting a good well-rounded education. Keep those grades up; stay involved in extracurricular activities. You learn a lot of leadership skills that way.

Good luck in your research project.

Sincerely,

Earnie Deavenport

"Know yourself. Focus on using your strengths and talents and learn how to delegate your weaknesses. [Know that] others have great ideas and different talents."

—TOBY HYNES, PRESIDENT,
GULF STATES TOYOTA, HOUSTON, TX

"You can't do everything well. Pick the things that matter most and concentrate on getting better and better, little by little, at those things."

—REUBEN MARK, Chairman and CEO, Colgate-Palmolive Company, New York, NY

"DON'T TAKE YOURSELF TOO SERIOUSLY. LEARN TO LAUGH AT YOURSELF AND TO HONESTLY CRITIQUE YOUR OWN PERFORMANCE. ONLY BY PERSONALLY RECOGNIZING YOUR OWN SHORTCOMINGS WILL YOU BE ABLE TO SHOW A LONG-TERM PATTERN OF CONTINUOUS IMPROVEMENT. WHEN THINGS DON'T GO RIGHT, DON'T GIVE UP. STUDY WHAT WENT WRONG AND THEN SHOW THAT YOU CAN RECOVER FROM A SETBACK."

—ROY W. HALEY, CEO, Wesco International, Pittsburgh, PA

Question & Answer

Q: What do I need to know beyond books and academics to become a leader?

A: Confidence counts. If you don't think you can do it, you'll be right 100% of the time. Focus on the job you have. Do it well, and others will notice your abilities. Then, new opportunities will come your way. . . . Companies are democracies. Real leaders aren't picked by their bosses. Their bosses only pick them after the true leaders have been identified by their peers.

—JOSEPH M. TUCCI, PRESIDENT AND CEO, EMC
CORP., HOPKINTON, MA

COLGATE-PALMOLIVE COMPANY
A Delaware Corporation

300 Park Avenue
New York, NY 10022

Reuben Mark
Chairman and Chief Executive Officer

May 19, 2003

Mr. Douglas Barry

Voorhes, New Jersey 08043

Dear Douglas:

Thank you for your recent letter and your interest in Colgate.

We spend considerable time and effort at our company helping Colgate people become better leaders, so your questions about leadership are ones we have considered over a long time.

Here are a few of the qualities we think you, or anyone, should have as a leader:

<u>Integrity</u> - Stand up for what's right, in small matters and large ones, and always do what you promise. The first requires common sense; the second requires good systems (sometimes as simple as a notebook for reminders) to ensure you follow-up on all your commitments.

<u>Focus</u> – you can't do everything well. Pick the things that matter most and concentrate on getting better and better, little by little, at those things.

<u>Inspire Others</u> – The best way to have others join in supporting your goals is to care about them as people and demonstrate your respect for them. We like to say that "Love is a better motivator than fear."

Recycled Paper

<u>Communicate simply</u> – A leader's job is to clarify and
simplify so that everyone understands what's truly important.
Express your ideas in terms everyone can grasp. No one can
follow a road map they can't read.

I hope you keep up your interest in leadership and apply what
you're learning in whatever field excites you most.

Best regards,

Experience the Bad and the Good

"Life is not a 'big bang theory' or a string of incredible successes—one following another. Life is always a series of ups and downs, triumphs and failures. You may be successful if your triumphs simply outnumber your failures. But, in order to be successful, you must experience those failures and you must learn from them."

—ERROLL B. DAVIS, JR., CHAIRMAN, PRESIDENT AND CEO, ALLIANT ENERGY CORP., MADISON, WI

THE DOCUMENT COMPANY
XEROX

G. Richard Thoman
President and Chief Executive Officer
Xerox Corporation
800 Long Ridge Road
Stamford, CT 06904

January 10, 1999

Mr. Douglas Barry

Voorhees, NJ 08043

Dear Douglas,

Thanks for your letter. You referred to yourself as "ambitious", so I believe you have already demonstrated one key attribute of becoming a CEO.

A few others high on the list would be:

- A good education and a willingness to devote yourself to a lifetime of learning. The world is constantly changing and the pace of that change is increasing geometrically. You will have to continue to learn and change and grow.

- A sense of balance in your life. Hard work, of course, is critical. But you have to balance that with time for your family and friends. One-dimensional people are rarely successful over the long haul.

- Problem-solving. People who go the furthest in their careers are people who can identify problems and come up with creative solutions.

I hope this is helpful. Good luck in school.

Sincerely,

G. Richard Thoman

GRT/khm

THE
DOCUMENT
COMPANY
XEROX
Worldwide Sponsor

ITOCHU Corporation
5-1, Kita-Aoyama 2-chome,
Minato-ku, Tokyo 107-8077, Japan

UICHIRO NIWA
President & C. E. O.

July 1, 2003

Mr. Douglas Barry

Voorhees, NJ 08043
USA

Dear Doug,

Thank you very much for your letter of June 17, asking for my advice on how you can reach your goal of becoming a CEO in the future. As Mr. Millard Drexler of GAP said in his letter to you, I don't know all the answers either. But, I believe that I can offer you some advice, which I hope might help you in your future endeavors.

The very first thing I want you to have is a strong and firm belief in yourself and in whatever you do. Belief in yourself is very important, because, without it, you can neither impress nor persuade people. When you have a strong belief in yourself, the sky is the limit for you and your future is as big as your imagination. But, remember that your belief must be backed up and supplemented by your constant efforts, whether it be in study or in business.

The second thing I would like to share with you is the importance of being humble. What I mean by "humble" is not being obsequious, but that you listen to others' opinions respectfully. During the course of my life, I have encountered many people who were very confident of themselves without listening to others. Those people invariably failed in whatever they did. We call them "self-centered". So, I would like you to become a person who understands clearly what is "self-confident" and what is "self-centered". This is the very point that could make or break your life.

The third point I would like to make is how you deal with yourself in times of adversity. As you go into the world, you will surely experience both good and bad times. I had my share of adversities, the biggest of which occurred when I was a food commodity trader in our New York office in the early 1970s. I made a loss of about one hundred million dollars and I almost quit the company. But, I was so determined to recoup the loss and, thanks to a cooperative climate back then, I was able to make more than enough to recoup the loss and to make a huge profit as well. Looking back, maybe, I was a little overconfident, but I didn't panic and lose my composure. But, still, it was not enough for me to just recoup the loss. Back then, I felt a God-like presence which totally embraced me, something beyond the reach of human power. This experience was a real eye-opener for me and I felt that I was blessed by the God who always watches me. I want you to know that so far as you do your best in whatever you do, somebody somewhere is always watching you and will reward you accordingly.

I hope that you find my observations helpful and instructive. I sincerely wish you every success in your future endeavors. Good luck!

Sincerely yours,

Uichiro Niwa
President & C.E.O.
ITOCHU Corporation

"Nothing in the competitive world of business is easy, but accomplishment usually results from knowing what you want to achieve and not giving up when inevitable obstacles get in the way."

—JAMES M. ZIMMERMAN, CHAIRMAN AND CEO, FEDERATED DEPARTMENT STORES INC., CINCINNATI, OH

"EXPECT THAT THINGS WILL WORK OUT OKAY (AND THEN WORK TO MAKE SURE THEY DO)."

—REUBEN MARK, Chairman and CEO, Colgate-Palmolive Co., New York, NY

"HARD WORK, OF COURSE, IS CRITICAL. BUT YOU HAVE TO BALANCE THAT WITH TIME FOR YOUR FAMILY AND FRIENDS. ONE-DIMENSIONAL PEOPLE ARE RARELY SUCCESSFUL OVER THE LONG HAUL."

—G. RICHARD THOMAN, President and CEO, Xerox Corp., Stamford, CN

Bossidy's Top 12

Lawrence A. Bossidy, CEO of Allied Signal, a Fortune 500 company in Morristown, NJ, succinctly profiled the necessary qualities of a CEO as follows:

1. Energy
2. Enthusiasm
3. Communication skills
4. Persuasion skills
5. Passion
6. Invincible determination
7. Disciplined
8. Decisive
9. Focused
10. Ego containment
11. Candor
12. Self confidence

JOHN T. DILLON
CHAIRMAN
AND CHIEF EXECUTIVE OFFICER

TWO MANHATTANVILLE ROAD
PURCHASE NY 10577

February 3, 2000

Mr. Douglas Barry

Voorhees, NJ 08043

Dear Douglas:

Thank you for your letter dated January 14, 2000 asking me to identify two or three qualities that will best prepare you to become a CEO.

There are many qualities a person needs to become a leader. The three traits I believe will help you to become a CEO are:
- Absolute dedication to excellence
- Trust in others and belief in team work
- No excuses - meet promises

Douglas, keep up the good work and keep challenging yourself. You may one day become a CEO. I wish you all the best in your life.

Sincerely,

John T. Dillon

"My policy has always been 'do your job as good as you can and the future will take care of itself.'"

—CARLOS M. GUTIERREZ, Chairman and CEO, Kellogg Company, Battle Creek, MI

"One must have self confidence but be humble enough to realize that true success is the ability to harness the best ideas of the team."

—R. KEITH ELLIOTT, CHAIRMAN,
HERCULES INC., WILMINGTON, DE

"You need to know yourself and you need to be comfortable in your own space, first and foremost."

—JUDITH M. VON SELDENECK, Chairman,
The Diversified Search Companies, Philadelphia, PA

Don H. Davis, Jr.
Chairman of the Board and
Chief Executive Officer

777 East Wisconsin Avenue, Suite 1400
Milwaukee, WI 53202

Rockwell

January 28, 2000

Mr. Douglas Barry

Voorhees, New Jersey 08043

Dear Douglas:

Thank you for your letter of January 14th. I am delighted to hear that you are already setting ambitious goals for your future. From reviewing your resume, it appears that you currently have achieved a good balance between education, music, sports, and hobbies. Continuing this balance throughout your life will help you in whatever field of business you ultimately pursue. As a Chief Executive Officer, I work hard to maintain balance between my career, my family, my community, and my hobbies. This balance has always provided me with the foundation that helped me achieve my potential.

If I identify, as requested, the three qualities that best prepared me to become a CEO, they would be as follows:

- <u>Unquestionable integrity</u>
  - Always take the high road.
  - Admit your mistakes and immediately make attempts to rectify them.
  - Don't say one thing, and do something else.

- <u>Customer focus</u>
  - Learn to be a good listener.
  - Value and respect the opinions of others.
  - Ask questions (e.g., who, what, where, when, why)

- <u>Perseverance</u>
  - Be passionate about what you do.
  - Go the extra mile to achieve your goals.
  - Enjoy competition and have a desire to win.

Page Two

I hope this information will provide some benefit to you as you look toward the future. I wish you every success. I'm sure your Mom and Dad are extremely proud of you.

Enclosed find a copy of Rockwell's Annual Report, the Rockwell Data Book, a recent brochure which overviews our businesses and global locations, and a copy of my public biography. For more information about Rockwell, you may visit our website at www.rockwell.com.

Very truly yours,

Don H. Davis, Jr.

enclosures

"I never take myself too seriously, and I oftentimes look at myself and this world as a distant observer. Believe me, there is a lot to laugh about."

—LEONARD RIGGIO, Chairman and CEO, Barnes & Noble, Inc., New York, NY

"The best thing that you can do right now is keep yourself open to a variety of experiences and not be afraid to make some mistakes."

—HENRY A. MCKINNELL, CHAIRMAN AND CEO, PFIZER INC., NEW YORK, NY

"I TRY TO DO MY HOMEWORK, AND THEN MAKE DECISIONS FASTER, RATHER THAN SLOWER."

—SANFORD I. WEILL, Chairman and Co-CEO, Citigroup Inc., New York, NY

The Importance of Being Humble

"[Some]thing I would like to share with you is the importance of being humble. What I mean by 'humble' is not being obsequious, but that you listen to others' opinions respectfully. During the course of my life, I have encountered many people who were very confident of themselves without listening to others. Those people invariably failed in whatever they did."

—VICHIRO NIWA, PRESIDENT AND CEO,
ITOCHU CORPORATION, TOKYO, JAPAN

What I've Learned

I never dreamed that these people who are so successful could possibly be so humble.

I reasoned that the most successful people in business, the CEOs, should all be openly proud of their success because they have a right to be. Yet I've learned that even the best have room for improvement, and that the best of the best understand this.

Whenever I mess up, I get flustered and upset and I dwell on my mistake. But I have realized that, instead of dwelling on the bad, I should learn from it and laugh about it because that one occurrence is so infinitesimal in the grand scheme of things. Mr. Riggio surprised me by saying that he never took himself too seriously. He explained that he could look at his situation, at his world, as a "distant observer." I find that since I've come to understand this strength, I've been able to see things in a more comprehensive way. In seeing the big picture, you can understand just how small you really are, even if you are a great corporate success. By understand-

ing this, you can also understand that the little failures along the way are not necessarily bad things
because they allow you to make room for improvement and they let you know that, after all, you're still
only human.

"Knowing what you don't know", as Mr. Barrett
said, is an essential quality for a good leader. There
isn't a person alive who knows every single thing,
and by understanding that you do not know certain
things, you can better prepare yourself to learn
them. Finding out who I am has been part of my
growth, and the more I find out about myself, the
better prepared I am to become the best I can be.
Doing things you don't necessarily like hides your
true self, and so the more you know what your likes
and dislikes are, what your strengths and your
weaknesses are, the easier you will be able to carve
out your own path to a successful and happy life. Mr.
Elliott wisely stated that a leader has to be both humble and confident because confidence reflects that
you believe in what you're doing but humility lets
you recognize the other ideas and opinions that are
floating around out there. In a lifetime, you will have
various ups and downs. But it is important to keep
everything in perspective, because your failures can
be turned into successes.

Index